MODELLING RAILWAYS IN
O GAUGE

MODELLING RAILWAYS IN
O GAUGE

JOHN EMERSON

THE CROWOOD PRESS

First published in 2016 by
The Crowood Press Ltd
Ramsbury, Marlborough
Wiltshire SN8 2HR

www.crowood.com

British Library Cataloguing-in-Publication Data
A catalogue record for this book is available from the British Library.

ISBN 978 1 78500 254 0

Acknowledgements
My thanks to Paul Bason, Dave Brewer of Tower Models, Mrs Helen Bright (grand-daughter-in-
law of W.S. Norris), Dave Coasby, Brian Daly, Steve Flint of the *Railway Modeller*, Pat Hammond,
Ben Jones of *British Railway Modelling*, Chris Klein of Ixion and Minerva Models, Peter Marriott,
the late Peter Marshall, and Michael Price for their help and assistance and loan of photographs.
And to my late mother for buying that Hornby tinplate train set!

Frontispiece: Stanier 'Jubilee' Alberta waits for the road on the author's 'Gifford Street' fine scale
layout. One of the benefits of the 'senior scale' is the greater size and mass of models – rolling
stock moves in a much more realistic manner than in the smaller scales. (Tony Wright, courtesy
British Railway Modelling)

Disclaimer
The author and the publisher do not accept any responsibility in any manner whatsoever for any
error or omission, or any loss, damage, injury, adverse outcome, or liability of any kind incurred
as a result of the use of any of the information contained in this book, or reliance upon it. If in
doubt about any aspect of railway modelling, readers are advised to seek professional advice.

Typeset and designed by D & N Publishing, Baydon, Wiltshire

Printed and bound in Malaysia by Times Offset (M) Sdn Bhd

CONTENTS

PREFACE

O gauge – the 'senior scale' – has been around for almost as long as the hobby of railway modelling and there is no denying that today, with the advent of high-quality ready-to-run locomotives and rolling stock, it is enjoying a huge surge in popularity. From the early days of methylated-spirit fired 'dribblers' and coarse-scale clockwork, railway modelling in 7mm scale has developed into one of the most popular and active branches of our hobby. Originally thought to be the smallest practical gauge for indoor model railways, and later seen as the province of only the very wealthy or the dedicated scratch-builder, O gauge now enjoys wide trade support with a huge range of kits and accessories, as well as an ever-growing number of ready-to-run models making it easily accessible to modellers (and non-modellers) from all kinds of backgrounds.

A commonly held but mistaken belief amongst modellers in the lesser scales is that O gauge is 'too expensive'. Given the spiralling cost of the average OO- or N-gauge model – especially if fitted with Digital Command Control (DCC) sound – there is no reason why a small O-gauge layout should cost much more than a OO layout built in a similar amount of space. And with the introduction of small O-gauge ready-to-run locomotives such as Dapol's immensely popular 'Terrier', Ixion's Hudswell Clarke 0-6-0ST or the Minerva 'E' Class Peckett 0-4-0ST, all currently priced at around £200, O gauge is easily within the reach of the average modeller's pocket. As with all things, your hobby will cost you just as much as you can afford to spend on it. Larger manufacturers are also keen to invest in the future of ready-to-run O gauge – Peco has recently introduced a new range of Setrack for O gauge, whilst Heljan has cornered the market in British outline ready-to-run diesel locomotives with its first steam outline locomotive planned for release in 2017. No wonder so many are now actively switching from the smaller scales and opting for O gauge.

By necessity, this book focuses on my experience of British outline fine-scale O gauge, gained through my own layout. By any stretch of the imagination, 'Gifford Street' is a big layout, but, like the majority of model railways of all scales and gauges, it began in a very small way and with a limited amount of equipment. Given the usual household demands on space, time and available disposable income, it was also built over a period of several years and, most importantly, constrained within a modest budget. But this is by no means the whole story, as the O-gauge modelling fraternity encompasses standard gauge, narrow and broad gauges and overseas prototypes, as well as electric, steam and spring-driven (clockwork) coarse-scale tinplate. The 7mm modeller can choose from modelling standards ranging from vintage and reproduction coarse scale through fine scale to the advanced standards of Scale7 or Proto48.

Whilst I make no claims that this is an exhaustive or comprehensive directory of O-gauge goods and services or modelling techniques, I hope new and not so new modellers wishing to model in 7mm scale will find it a useful primer, with more than enough information and inspiration to set them well on the road to enjoying the benefits of the senior scale. Such is the growth of modern ready-to-run standard and narrow-gauge models that it can rightly be said that there has never been a better time to be an O-gauge modeller – and with the world of O gauge now open to modellers of all abilities and from all walks of life, it is time to dispel that most commonly held myth – 'I can't afford O gauge … !'

John Emerson
'Gifford Street'
February 2016

CHAPTER ONE

INTRODUCING O GAUGE

Dawn of the diesels – the six-car Midland Pullman, a regular and much requested performer on 'Gifford Street' at exhibitions. Built from Westdale kits by Richard Dockerill and powered by twin ABC motor bogies, the two power cars are fitted with DCC sound decoders specially blown by South West Digital.
TONY WRIGHT, COURTESY BRITISH RAILWAY MODELLING

A PERSONAL JOURNEY

'Gifford Street' is only the second O-gauge layout that I have been involved with after taking the decision to move up in scale from OO gauge, although it has gone through several stages of evolution over many years. Like most of my generation, my introduction to the world of model trains began in the 1950s

with a Hornby O-gauge tinplate clockwork train set one Christmas. Bearing little relationship to any full-size engines or rolling stock and hurtling around coarse-scale tinplate track at horrendous speed – on the dining table or out in the garden – it was a world away from the highly detailed models that now run on 'Gifford Street'. Nevertheless, those colourful tin printed toys from Binns Road fired my young

The fascination of tinplate trains – Hornby O-gauge in Grandmother's garden circa 1956.

imagination, sowing the seeds of a lifelong interest in railways and the hobby of model railways in general. Following many years working in 4mm scale (from three-rail Hornby-Dublo to dabbling in P4), a series of incomplete layout projects culminated in the 4mm-scale modern-image diesel exhibition layout 'Hayley Mills'. But after several years on the exhibition circuit in the 1980s, the O-gauge bug bit – and when it does bite, it bites hard! Following in the footsteps of many other railway modellers, the 4mm layout and stock were sold and the move up to the senior scale began in earnest.

The relative size of the same model in O, OO and N gauge.

While each scale and gauge used by railway modellers has its own obvious merits and attractions, there are many benefits from making the move to modelling in O gauge. First and perhaps most obvious is size – you simply get more bang for your buck! The larger size means that it is not only easier to build O-gauge models, but also simpler to add fine detail, while for older modellers O gauge is much easier on the eyes. The greater mass and weight of O gauge means that rolling stock will roll in a more realistic manner and make a more realistic sound clattering over track joints, points and crossings. Larger models have more space inside in which to fit DCC decoders, loudspeakers, smoke units, lights and working fans for diesels. Most importantly, for a given area you may not actually need as much track and equipment as in the smaller scales, so overall the cost can be comparable, if not less. Finally, the sheer size makes owning and handling O-gauge models a much more enjoyable experience.

WHAT IS O GAUGE?

Put simply, most modellers think of O gauge as modelling to a scale of 7mm to the foot (expressed as a scale ratio of 1:43.5), with a track gauge of 32mm. However, this only covers standard gauge (4ft 8½in, or 1,435mm) in the UK and there are a variety of scales and gauges grouped together under the generic term 'O gauge', a term used throughout this book. More than a century of sometimes erratic progress has seen modern high-tech O gauge evolve from what were little more than crude toys, referred to solely by 'gauge' – the term 'scale' as railway modellers understand it today being virtually unknown. Although there were no set standards, from as early as 1891 pioneering German toy manufacturer Märklin had produced models in a series of numbered gauges. For the more affluent, reasonably 'scale' working steam locomotives were available in the larger gauges for running outdoors, while Gauge No.1 was seen as a small gauge suitable for indoor use. Gauge No.0 (nought or zero) was something of an afterthought and at the time considered the smallest practical scale. By 1899, a list of standards for model railways, including Gauge 0, had been published in the *Model Engineer* by the newly formed Society of Model Engineers (see Table 1). Most models were either steam or clockwork driven, as electrically powered traction, both prototype and model, was still in its infancy – and with no nationwide domestic electricity supply and few electric motors small or reliable enough, most electrically driven models were powered either by batteries or accumulators.

Whilst these early standards proposed a fixed scale and track gauge, they did not address the issue of back-to-back or other critical dimensions. Henry Greenly and W.J. Bassett-Lowke jointly published a set of standard dimensions for model and miniature railways in 1909, which largely remained in use, with additions and alterations, until the British Railway Modelling Standards Bureau (BRMSB) laid down its preferred standards in the 1940s (see Table 2).

Table 1	1899 Standards for Model Railway Gauges Nos 0–4				
Gauge	**Scale**	**Ratio**	**Track Gauge**	**Notes**
No.4	⅘in	1:15	3in	Largest of the model railway gauges – now obsolete
No.3	½in	1:22	2½in	Still in use today supported by Gauge 3 Association
No.2	7/16in	1:27	2½in	Track gauge altered to 2in in 1909 – now defunct
No.1	10mm	1:36	1¾in	Still in use today, supported by GIMRA
No.0	7mm	1:44	1¼in	Track gauge half that of No.3 gauge – now known as O gauge

Table 2 BRMSB Dimensions for 'Standard' O Gauge	
(Taken from *Model Railway Constructor*, October 1944)	
Gauge (straight track)	32mm
Flangeway (straight track)	2.5mm
Flangeway (curved track)	3mm
Flange thickness (nominal)	1.5mm
Back-to-back (permanent way)	28mm
Back-to-back (tinplate track)	27mm
Rail height	5mm
Rail width	2mm

GOLDEN AGE OF COARSE SCALE

W.J. Bassett-Lowke is generally credited with being the 'father of the model railway hobby' in the UK and in 1902 he began importing large-scale models made by the German firms of Märklin, Bing and Carette. Following strong anti-German sentiment in the UK after World War I, toy manufacturers were urged to 'produce clockwork trains to replace those which used to be imported from the continent'. Although Bassett-Lowke continued to import German mechanisms, the company also began manufacturing more items, especially in the smaller and increasingly popular gauge 0.

From 1933 to the outbreak of World War II in 1939, Bassett-Lowke produced high-specification hand-built models of locomotives powered by clockwork or electric (8–10V DC or 20V AC), although these were well beyond the pocket of the average enthusiast. It was laughingly said that if your father worked in a bank, you would have a Hornby train for Christmas, but if your father was the bank manager, then you could expect Bassett-Lowke! However, over the years Bassett-Lowke produced some classic and now highly collectable models, including a Stanier 2-cylinder 2-6-4T, LMS 'Compound' and 2P 4-4-0, GWR 'Castle' and a prototype 'Deltic'. The business gradually declined post-war, until ceasing in 1965. The Bassett-Lowke name was eventually acquired by Corgi in 1996, with the Corgi empire being taken over by Hornby in 2008.

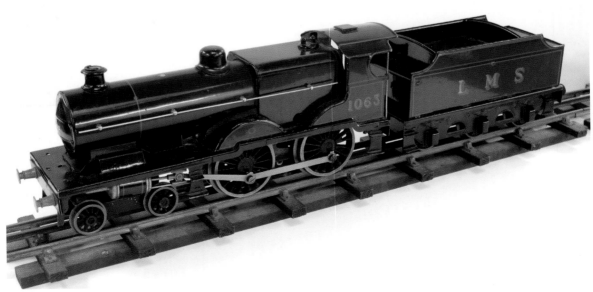

Period piece from the 1930s – a Bassett-Lowke 12V DC three-rail LMS 'Compound'.

Other significant O-gauge manufacturers of the time included the Leeds Model Company, producing the third largest range of O-gauge models. Established by Rex Stedman, it was one of the first manufacturers to use early plastics (Bakelite) for proprietary models. Mills Brothers (Milbro), Bonds and Edward Exley, who produced most of the coaches for the Bassett-Lowke range, were amongst other well-known names. There were also many smaller, less well-known but equally important makes, such as the Windsor Model Co., Douglass Models and R. Models of Cheltenham.

HORNBY CLOCKWORK TRAINS 'O' GAUGE

YOUNG BOYS find endless delight and satisfaction in all that a Hornby Clockwork Railway has to offer. Hornby Locomotives with their powerful long-running clockwork mechanisms are part of a model railway system which includes a fine selection of track, rolling stock and accessories—all sturdily constructed to last for years.

One of the attractions of a Hornby Clockwork railway is being able to start in a small way with a train and track, and then add to the equipment from time to time. The choice of Hornby trains ensures reliable performance, all components being tested and guaranteed before despatch from the Meccano Works.

No. 20 GOODS TRAIN SET
Contains No. 20 Locomotive (non-reversing), No. 20 Tender, two No. 20 Wagons and Rails.

No. 21 PASSENGER TRAIN SET
Contains No. 20 Locomotive (non-reversing), No. 20 Tender, two No. 21 Coaches and Rails.

Train Sets No. 20, 21, 30 and 31 are supplied with 1 ft. radius rails requiring a space of 3 ft. 3 in. by 2 ft. 6 in. Train Sets No. 41 and 45 are supplied with 2 ft. radius rails requiring a space of 5 ft. 4 in. by 4 ft. 6 in.

14

No. 30 GOODS TRAIN SET
Contains No. 30 Locomotive (reversing), No. 30 Tender, No. 30 Wagon, No. 30 Goods Van and Rails.

No. 31 PASSENGER TRAIN SET
Contains No. 30 Locomotive (reversing), No. 30 Tender, No. 31 Coach 1st/2nd, No. 31 Coach Brake/2nd and Rails.

No. 45 TANK GOODS TRAIN SET
Contains No. 40 Tank Locomotive (reversing), No. 50 Wagon, No. 50 Lumber Wagon, No. 50 "SHELL" Tank Wagon and Rails.

No. 41 TANK PASSENGER TRAIN SET
Contains No. 40 Tank Locomotive (reversing), two No. 41 Coaches, No. 41 Passenger Brake Van and Rails.

15

Post-war Hornby O gauge – whilst tinplate and clockwork had a charm of its own, it could no longer compete with the smaller, more realistic OO-gauge electric-powered trains.

But the golden age of coarse-scale O gauge was dominated by one name – Hornby. Frank Hornby had founded Meccano Ltd in 1908 and in 1920 introduced the first in what was to become the world-famous gauge-O Hornby Trains. Whilst most of the locomotives were of freelance design, there were several of more prototypical appearance, such as the later No.2 Special 4-4-0s and *Princess Elizabeth*, but all were designed for coarse-scale operation. Production stopped during World War II and when it resumed in 1946 the range had been greatly reduced. It has been suggested that Hornby was responsible for the term 'O gauge' replacing 'gauge 0' as a result of branding its OO-gauge tabletop model railway 'Dublo', although the term seems to have been used in the model press for some while previously. However, Hornby's strong advertising and publicity presence, as well as its pricing and marketing strategy, ensured that Hornby O gauge remained a market leader until sales declined in the 1950s and the Meccano empire collapsed in 1965.

Even Hornby's sought-after *Princess Elizabeth* was hardly a 'scale' model, so for the aspiring schoolboy enthusiast who could not afford Bassett-Lowke, or the 'average modeller' who wanted to build a more accurate scale model, the alternative was to scratch-build. Nevertheless, some notable layouts appeared in the inter-war years, including the Rev. Thomas Bernard Parley's outdoor line, G.P. Keen's 'K' Lines, Norman Eagle's 'Sherwood Section of the LMS' and Jack Ray's 'Crewchester', but most were to coarse-scale standards and many still relied on clockwork power.

However, there were fine-scale pioneers promoting finer standards for gauge O and names such as Col G.G. Templar, Bernard Miller, James Beeson and W.S. Norris began to appear in the model press arguing the case for a fine-scale approach. According to the late Jack Ray, at the age of twelve Norris was 'turning out models which would do credit to a man twice that age'. Dissatisfied with the crude standard of track then available, Norris also had his own special bullhead-section rail drawn and accurate cast chairs produced in the 1920s. From the 1930s, he contributed letters, photographs and articles to the *Model Railway Constructor* and *Model Railway News*,

'Star' Class 4-6-0 No.4053 **Princess Alexandria** *at the head of an Ocean Mails special on the three-rail GWR layout of fine-scale pioneer W.S. Norris, sometime in the 1930s. This photograph appeared on the cover of the Rocket Precision catalogue.*

edited by his great friend and fellow fine-scale proponent, John Neville Maskelyne. Norris, along with G. P. Keen and Captain W.F.P. Kelly, was also the driving force behind the Rocket Precision 'Scaleoh' range, producing components for fine-scale O gauge and with a photograph of his three-rail layout appearing on the front cover of the catalogue.

SIXTY YEARS OF THE SENIOR SCALE

Despite developments by these early fine-scale pioneers, it would take many years for O gauge to shake off its coarse-scale 'toy train' image. Midway through the twentieth century, O gauge all but disappeared due to the rise in popularity of the ready-to-run tabletop scales, more suited to the smaller room sizes of houses being built in the post-war reconstruction. According to the late George Hinchcliffe, just nine companies produced items for O-gauge modellers in the 1950s and grave concerns were being expressed about the lack of offerings from the trade. There was a very real threat to the continued existence of O gauge, even as a scratch-builder's medium.

There was certainly very little on offer. For example, the *Railway Modeller* for 1956 contained little of interest for the O-gauge modeller: two features on Cyril Fry's spectacular Irish International Railway and Tramway system; a scratch-built spring-driven (clockwork) Midland Railway 0-4-0T for the Sherwood Section described by Norman Eagles; and an SR (ex-LSWR) well wagon built by E.B. Trotter. Trade news was virtually non-existent, with only a mention of two-rail as a new development for Bassett-Lowke, and photographs of two superbly built locomotives commissioned from Edward Exley, who also had an advertisement.

Letters by Harold Bower and others in the model press suggested the formation of a gauge-O association 'similar to that which has done such excellent work in gauge one' and led to the founding of the Gauge O Guild in 1956. In the same year, W.S. Norris moved to Chilworth in Surrey, where construction of a new two-rail fine-scale layout started in a 70 × 22ft (21.3 × 6.7m) purpose-built shed. Dubbed

by J.N. Maskelyne as 'Britain's finest layout', it is hard to imagine the impact it had when first revealed to an unsuspecting readership in the June 1957 issue of *Model Railway News*. Maskelyne went on to describe the layout in further issues of *MRN* as 'the new deal for O gauge', which it certainly must have seemed at the time.

In the October 1957 issue of *Railway Modeller*, Cyril Freezer noted a significant number of new 7mm-scale models on static display stands at exhibitions – members of the new Guild flying the flag perhaps – adding that pre-war, the LNER had assembled a collection of 7mm models for a proposed exhibition layout. British Railways went on to develop its own O-gauge travelling layouts, which between 1948 and 1966 became a popular attraction up and down the country.

However, the post-war period was still an age of old-fashioned litho-printed tinplate, coarse-scale clockwork drive and three-rail or stud-contact electric models. Although plastic injection-moulding was in its infancy, long-established concerns such as CCW were still producing wooden coach and wagon kits for the OO- and O-gauge modeller, long after Kitmaster and Airfix had introduced their OO-gauge plastic construction kits. Even with the encouragement of the newly established Gauge O Guild, only a handful of loco kits were on offer. The 1962 Ian Allan *abc of Model Railways* included just five manufacturers in its list of available O-gauge locomotives: Bassett-Lowke; Bonds (both ready-to-run); CCW (white metal); Dawson (tinplate or nickel silver); and Douglass Models (loco bodies mainly in 'Bondaglass' fibreglass resin). Any rivet detail had to be marked out and punched by the purchaser prior to assembly. By the end of the 1960s, the Gauge O Guild was still trying to convince the trade and trade press that 'interest is far from dying out in gauge O and is, in fact, increasing'. But those who wanted mass-produced ready-to-run O gauge would have to wait a decade after the formation of the Gauge O Guild before anything appeared in any quantity, and not until the end of the twentieth century could O-gauge modellers enjoy ready-to-run models of a similar standard to those produced in the smaller gauges.

From 1948 until as late as 1966, British Railways exhibited several O-gauge layouts around the country showing the latest developments in motive power and freight handling. Much of the locomotives and rolling stock was built in BR's own workshops.
JOHN EMERSON COLLECTION

Gauge O was given a huge boost in 1966 with the appearance of Tri-ang's Big Big range. The battery-powered 'Blue Flyer' locomotive was a virtually scale model of the Western Region 'Hymek' diesel-hydraulic, so it was not long before modellers were converting it to 12V DC operation. According to Pat Hammond in *The Story of Rovex*, in excess of 150,000 of the blue and white version were produced, with a further 16,500 produced in 1970 in a particularly horrible bright yellow, red and black livery. Rolling stock comprised a

O-gauge pioneers – Tri-ang Big Big mineral wagons have been used on O-gauge layouts for the best part of half a century. These two survivors have replacement metal wheels and simple hook and loop couplings.

16 ton mineral wagon and semi-scale Mk2 coach; other rolling stock was based on Continental or American-inspired prototypes. A Ruston 0-4-0 diesel shunter and side-tipping wagon were also part of the Big Big range. Designed by Raphael Lipkin (Toys) Limited, part of the Lines Group, and based on narrow-gauge prototypes adapted to run on O-gauge track, they were originally intended as an entirely separate range, but made ideal conversion projects for modellers of large-scale narrow-gauge railways. Well over 120,000 locos and 274,000 wagons were produced and sold worldwide until production ceased in 1972.

The Big Big tooling was acquired by Novo Toys in 1975 and further production continued until 1980. However, in 1967 the Big Big concept had also been licensed to Italian company Lima and marketed as their Jumbo range. From 1973, Lima went on to produce its own models, including a 4F 0-6-0 (1975), a Class 33 diesel (1977); Mk1 coaches, 16 ton mineral and open wagons and a 'Toad' Brake Van, although the locomotives and coaches at least were to a smaller scale than their 1:43 counterparts. This did not deter enthusiastic modellers from converting the coaches to a more 'scale' appearance, while

Dismissed by many as under-scale toys, the Lima Class 33 has formed the basis for many conversions into detailed scale models since its introduction in 1977. This fine example is the work of skilled model-maker Richard Dockerill.

the 4F formed the basis of many ingenious projects to turn it into a convincing variety of locomotive types. Production continued until the early 1980s, although batches of the Class 33 and Mk1 coaches appeared in 1991 and 1999/2000. Following the collapse of Lima in 2004, Hornby acquired the Lima assets, although it has no plans to reissue any of the old O-gauge range.

While the formation of the Protofour Society in 1969 put 4mm fine-scale modelling firmly centre stage, the gauge-O fraternity seemed more concerned with the search for a manufacturer of replacement springs for obsolescent clockwork mechanisms. This half a century after Norris had begun promulgating fine-scale standards for O gauge! However, the winds of change finally began to blow through the 1970s, when firms such as Three Aitch Mouldings started to produce injection-moulded plastic wagon kits and Slater's, well known for its 'Huminiatures' and pioneering use of 'Plastikard', also began to produce plastic kits for O-gauge wagons. Today, Slater's produces more than seventy wagon kits covering a wide variety of freight subjects as well as locomotives and coaching stock.

A rather incomplete example of an early O-gauge plastic cattle wagon kit produced by Three Aitch Mouldings.

Slater's BR 12T Meat Van (7065), BR 20T Brake Van (7033), BR 12T 'Vanwide' (7062), and BR 13T 'Conflat' A (7067) and Type A Container (706A), all in regular use on 'Gifford Street'.

The development of etched kits can be traced back to the 1940s and 1950s when Sayer Chaplin produced its 4mm range, although these were little more than engraved parts that the purchaser then had to fret out. However, the process of producing etched-brass kits had advanced tremendously by 1976 when Metal Models released a superb highly detailed etched-brass kit of the GWR 'Siphon F', a benchmark model still comparable with anything produced today. At the same time, David Parkins began producing etched-brass kits of rolling stock and diesel locomotives, later acquired by Colonel Ronnie Hoare under the RJH label. For many years, these were the mainstay of 'modern-image' modellers, although they were not ideal, as forming flat metal into the subtle shapes of diesel locos was no easy task. However, some very impressive models could be the end result for those prepared to put in a lot of work.

In 1977, DJH began manufacturing white-metal 4mm-scale locomotive kits, moving into 7mm scale with the first composite white-metal/etched-brass kits produced in the UK, and later going on to produce diesel locomotives with one-piece pewter bodyshells. Around the same time, Colin Massingham began producing his MTK range, also moving into 7mm with kits covering locomotives, DMUs and EMU stock.

Although the quality was variable to say the least (with tongue very firmly in cheek, he rebranded them as the 'El Crappo' range), for many years these were the only source of kits for many diesel and electric prototypes. In complete contrast, London retailer Chuffs upped the game when it introduced its Sevenscale L&Y Pug locomotive kit in 1979. Complete with highly detailed white-metal castings for the body, robust brass chassis, wheels, motor and gears, couplings and even a bag of coal, this kit went on to gain a Design Centre Award and remains in production today, although now in the Springside range.

In the 1980s, Richard Webster introduced several finely moulded plastic kits of GWR prototypes under the Webster Developments label, including a tunnel van and Toad Brake Van. Later acquired by Peco, these kits are still in production alongside Peco's own 16 ton mineral, BR iron ore tippler and pig iron wagon kits. Towards the end of the 1980s, Richard Hollingworth and Andrew Hastie of Parkside Dundas introduced their first injection-moulded plastic kits for O gauge. Starting with three North British Railway prototypes acquired from Ian Kirk, this range has gone from strength to strength and, along with Slater's, has provided the backbone of freight stock on many O-gauge layouts for more than three

Etched and cast kits are a little more challenging – cast white-metal kits such as the 40T Warflat from ABS are best assembled with low-melt solder, although can also be successfully completed using suitable adhesives. Etched kits like the LNER 20T Tube by Connoisseur Models, 26T Trout ballast hopper from RJH, and LMS 10T Gunpowder van (Haywood Models) will require some experience with the soldering iron.

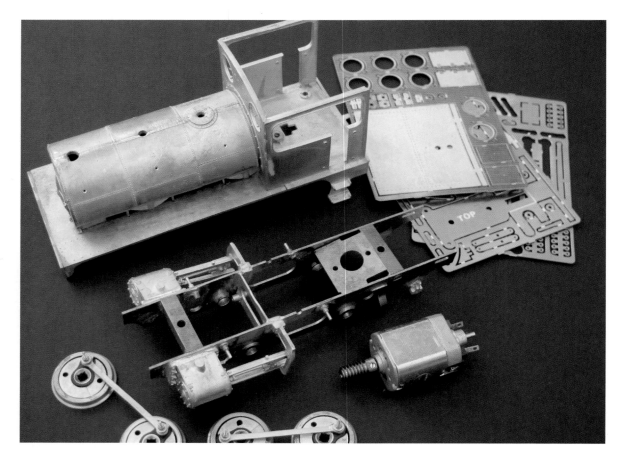

decades. A total of sixty-three wagon and van kits are now available in O gauge from Parkside, including pre-printed private owner wagons.

Amongst these pioneers were many other manufacturers producing O-gauge kits, regrettably far too many to list here – ABS, Freightman, Appleby Model Engineering, Vulcan, Eric Underhill and Jim Harris's Oakville range are just a few examples that spring to mind. Whilst some may have faded into obscurity, many of the various kit ranges have survived, although often having passed into different ownership.

However, it was record producer Pete Waterman who brought a fresh look at the whole business of producing kits for O-gauge modellers. Having already been involved in the production of kits for OO gauge in the 1970s and needing to

*ABOVE: **The award-winning L&Y Pug kit. Originally produced by Sevenscale, this is one of the later versions made by Springside Models.***

*LEFT: **Webster Developments GWR Tunnel Van and 12T Mink van later became part of the Peco range, which already included a kit for a 16T mineral wagon.***

Freightman kits were supplied either complete with underframe components from the ABS range of white-metal castings, or as body kits to fit Lima or Tri-ang wagon chassis. This is an SR 12T even-plank fitted van.

Several models under construction from the growing JLTRT range. The kits feature detailed high-impact resin body with underframe and detail fittings in white metal or lost-wax brass for easy assembly using suitable cyanoacrylate adhesives (superglue).

produce locomotives and rolling stock in a reasonably quick timescale for his 'Leamington Spa' project, Pete took the plunge into manufacturing once again with his Just Like The Real Thing range. Initially concentrating on diesel prototypes, JLTRT has grown to encompass diesel and steam locomotives, coaching and freight stock, as well as a range of building and other components, many originally designed for 'Leamington Spa', but added to the range to benefit other O-gauge modellers. Using innovative manufacturing methods such as CAD design, resin casting, 3D prototyping and laser-cutting, as well as the more traditional use of metal casting and etched-brass, the JLTRT range has taken O-gauge modelling into the twenty-first century.

THE RISE AND RISE OF RTR

The attraction of British O gauge has been further enhanced in recent years by the introduction of realistically priced ready-to-run (RTR) locomotives and rolling stock produced to a similar standard seen in OO- and N-gauge RTR models, a situation previously only enjoyed in the USA or on the Continent. Although these new-generation models employ modern production methods, they are manufactured in relatively small numbers compared to the mass OO-gauge market, so usually sell out quickly. A significant milestone on the road to modern O-gauge RTR came from Stephen J. Maris of Specialised Products. For many years, he had produced 'Waverley' fine-scale O-gauge point kits, but in 1990 announced a ready-to-run LMS 'Jinty' 0-6-0T, batch-built using resin cast, fibreglass and etched components. Finished in plain black, with compensated chassis, plunger-type pick-ups and jointed milled rods, the first batch of locomotives sold for just £160 plus post and packing, phenomenal value for such a well-designed model with superb running qualities. A further batch was advertised in the December 1990 issue of the Gauge O Guild *Gazette*.

Another model in development was based on the LMS 4F 0-6-0 and demonstrated at the Gauge O Guild Trade show at Bletchley, with an S&DJR 2-8-0 mooted as a possible follow-up. Sadly, Stephen Maris died before either project reached fruition, but the legacy of his RTR 'Jinty' had set a high standard for others to follow.

Around the same time, Martin Wynne of 85A Models had been developing a RTR Hunslet 15in 0-6-0ST, which appeared in 1993. This took a different approach to the Specialised Products 'Jinty', being a ready-assembled injection-moulded plastic model. Powered with a Mashima 1833 motor, 40:1 gearbox and split-axle pick-up, it was initially priced at £99, subsequently rising to a more realistic £140. From mid-1993, it was also available in kit form, comprising seven main body parts and factory-assembled plastic chassis for just £99. The all-plastic construction meant that no soldering was needed; only glue and paint were required to complete the locomotive. It was an ideal entry-level model for those wanting an inexpensive RTR locomotive, or wishing to build a locomotive for the first time, and was perfectly at home in an industrial or light railway setting. The last one was sold in 1998 and Martin went on to develop TemPlot, although examples still appear from time to time on the second-hand market.

Randolph Chang was a director of Bachmann until 1992, leaving to set up his own brass manufacturing company, San Cheng, and can be credited with

The RTR 'Jinty' produced by Specialised Products towards the end of the twentieth century significantly raised the bar for O-gauge RTR.

85A Models Hunslet **Airedale** *given a makeover by David L.O. Smith and described in the May 1999 issue of the Gauge O Guild's* **Gazette** *and also archived on David's website.*

establishing the contemporary fine-scale RTR O-gauge market. Bachmann introduced its Brassworks range in 1996, beginning with BR Mk1 coaches and followed in 1999 by a two-car Class 101 DMU and Class 24. Although advertised as ready-to-run, it was left to the purchaser to prepare and paint the models and to install seating and glazing, which were not supplied. Even so, for the price this was always going to be a good deal for the modeller. Early models had a lacquer finish that could affect paint adhesion if not thoroughly cleaned off, but was left off later models.

The coaching stock and locomotives proved popular, with the Class 08 diesel shunter reputedly being the bestseller, but sales of four-wheel tank wagons and MEA box wagons proved disappointing. Further locomotives were introduced, each one improving on the standards of earlier models, so that the final releases like the LMS 'Crab' were quite sophisticated models. A selection of models and their release dates include:

The Class 08 diesel shunter was the most successful model in the Bachmann Brassworks range, while the tank wagons and modern box wagons had disappointing sales figures.

Midland main-line power – all-brass 'Jubilee' and 'Patriot' models produced by San Cheng, both painted and lined by Warren Hayward. The 'Patriot' was the last model produced for the Tower Brass range.

BR Mk1 coaches (1996); Class 101 Metro-Cammell DMU (1999); J94 0-6-0ST (July 2005); LMS 4F 0-6-0 and J39 0-6-0 (September 2005); A3 4-6-2 including *Flying Scotsman* (April 2006); Class 03 0-6-0DM (May 2006); BR 4MT 2-6-4T (January 2008); Class 101 Metro-Cammell DMU (re-released May 2008); and LMS 2MT 2-6-0 (November 2008).

The advent of the Brassworks range added significantly to the development of O-gauge RTR and provided a huge shot in the arm for O-gauge modelling, encouraging many modellers lacking the time or skills to build a locomotive to enter the ranks of 7mm modellers for the first time. Where O gauge had previously been perceived as a medium mainly for scratch-builders, now it was possible for anyone to get a layout up and running in a reasonably short amount of time. San Cheng offered its production facilities to other concerns, including Blackpool-based Tower Models, which had acquired the remaining stocks and production rights to the Brassworks range after Bachmann decided to concentrate on OO and N gauge for the UK market. Once incorporated into its RTR Tower Brass range, Tower Models also began introducing its own new locomotives with further refinements and an increasing level of sophistication that had not previously been available in RTR brass.

New coaches including GWR 57ft (17.4m) Collett stock also appeared and the Bachmann Mk1 coaches were re-run at least once.

San Cheng had also begun introducing its own RTR brass-built locomotives, at first sold directly to the public but later through Leeds-based Finescale Brass as well as Tower Models. Both also offered fully finished locomotives in a choice of liveries off the shelf, or finished to specific requirements. When San Cheng finally ended production, it effectively brought to an end the era of relatively inexpensive RTR brass. Other names have entered the RTR brass market, including Golden Age Models, Laurie Loveless, Master Models, Sette Models, Masterpiece Models and Lee Marsh, offering fully finished locomotives and in some cases sets of coaches. However, the majority of these high-end RTR models can only be described as being of almost 'museum quality' and consequently are usually beyond the pocket of the average modeller.

O GAUGE – THE NEW N GAUGE

Skytrex had been producing military and naval scale models for a number of years and had also developed a range of N-gauge railway models. In 2004,

Skytrex introduced a range of robustly made RTR vans and wagons at attractive prices, including these Suncole Private Owner eight-plank wagons complete with coke raves.

the company decided to move into O gauge with a small but promising range of RTR injection-moulded plastic vans and wagons. The range expanded rapidly to include RTR locomotives and a DMU, all powered by excellent mechanisms from the Czech ETS range. But, partly due to overproduction, the company ultimately folded and remaining stocks were disposed of. However, the Skytrex name subsequently reap-

peared in 2013 and although no longer producing RTR locomotives, is once again enjoying considerable success.

However, it fell to Danish manufacturer Heljan really to kick-start the twenty-first century O-gauge RTR revolution with the first in a range of British diesel locomotives. These new-generation models featured a highly detailed injection-moulded plastic

A true workhorse – the Heljan Class 47 is a powerful RTR O-gauge locomotive at home on late steam-era layouts as well as all-diesel lines. This example is fitted with DCC sound.

body on a heavy cast-metal chassis with powerful twin motors. Ironically, Heljan's first model was a 'Hymek' (announced in 2004, but released November 2005), echoing the abortive entry by Rovex into the O-gauge market some forty years earlier. A Class 47 arrived in 2007, followed by a Class 37 (2008) and Class 20 (2009). The range has expanded to include a Class 60, modern air-braked freight rolling stock and steam locomotives.

After producing a series of GWR wagon kits in the 1980s, Richard Webster had gone on to join Bachmann, running the Kader factory in China for five years, before becoming Vice-President of Engineering for Lionel, America's oldest model train company. In 2009, he started Lionheart Trains, now taken over by Dapol, introducing a finely detailed RTR O-gauge GWR pannier tank, auto-coach (with DCC sound) and a range of freight rolling stock. The range is constantly growing, including GWR 'Small Prairie' tank and 'Mogul', seven-plank coal and coke wagons, and 14 ton Air Ministry tank wagons. Further planned models include a GWR 'B-Set', suburban coaches and a BR Standard 3MT 2-6-2T. A few years later, Anglo-Australian firm Ixion Models, which had already produced a diminutive Manning Wardle 0-4-0ST, released its RTR Hudswell Clarke 0-6-0ST, which proved a huge success. This was followed by a Fowler 0-4-0 diesel mechanical shunter in 2014. Although Ixion has since dropped out of the UK market, Chris Klein

joined forces with Chris Basten of Dragon Models to produce a RTR Peckett 0-4-0ST, Kerr-Stuart 0-6-0T and 57xx 0-6-0PT under the Minerva Models label.

Dapol had announced its intention to produce a RTR O-gauge range some time ago, but its eventual entry into the O-gauge arena has proved to be something of a protracted affair. Although some innovative manufacturing techniques were employed for the range of open wagons, early releases were criticized for errors, such as brake levers neither 'on' nor 'off', unprototypical arrangement of body-side strapping on the five-plank wagon, and generic six-wheel milk tanks that combine LMS and GWR features. Despite this, Dapol has gone on to assemble a great team, whose expertise should now take the company's products to a new level with a quality range of RTR O-gauge locomotives and rolling stock, including the Lionheart Range, now taken over by Dapol.

The distinction of being Dapol's first O-gauge RTR loco fell to the diminutive LBSCR/SR/BR A1/A1X 'Terrier' 0-6-0T, available in DC or DCC sound versions. This has rightly proved an immensely popular model, and O-gauge modellers are now looking forward to the arrival of the long awaited and completely redesigned Class 08 diesel shunter. At the time of writing, tooling is well advanced for the next generation of Dapol freight rolling stock, based on BR standard wagon types, and featuring diecast compensated chassis as well as a 57xx 0-6-0.

The DCC version of Lionheart Trains 64xx pannier tank, available in a variety of well-researched liveries. This example will be one of the locos on the successor layout to 'Gifford Street' and has ATC battery box and cab conduit fitted, together with a little added weathering.

Ixion Models' 18in Hudswell Clarke 0-6-0ST was supplied complete with etched-brass name and builder's plates, plus a set of plastic tools and fire irons. It proved so popular with O-gauge modellers that a further batch of models was produced in 2014.

Industrial action – Minerva Models 'E' Class Peckett 0-4-0ST, a familiar motive sight on the the Swansea Harbour Trust railway, although many more were employed in British industry. The detailed Minerva model includes original and GWR-style domes, extra toolboxes, workplates and add-on cab shutters.
COURTESY CHRIS KLEIN, MINERVA MODELS

Dapol's first O-gauge locomotive was the diminutive 'Terrier' 0-6-0T. It has proved hugely popular amongst O-gauge modellers. The long-awaited Class 08 diesel shunter finally made its appearance in 2016.
COURTESY DAPOL

An O-Gauge Timeline

1825	*Stockton & Darlington – the world's first public railway operated by steam locomotives*
1863	Frank Hornby born in Liverpool
1867	Henry Greenly born in Birkenhead
1877	W.J. Bassett-Lowke born in Northampton
1887	Bonds Ltd established
1892	*Abolition of the GWR broad gauge*
1899	Society of Model Engineers draws up list of standards for gauge Nos 0–4; Bassett-Lowke starts model engineering business
1901	Greenly appointed Assistant Editor of *The Model Engineer*
1907	Meccano trademark registered
1909	Bassett-Lowke and Greenly publish revised standards for model railways
1912	Rex Stedman establishes Leeds Model Company
1920	Frank Hornby introduces first O-gauge train set
1923	*The Grouping – Britain's railways amalgamate into the 'Big Four' (GWR, LMS, LNER and SR)*
1926	Bonds become Bonds O'Euston Road
1936	Frank Hornby dies, aged seventy-three
1937	Hornby introduces *Princess Elizabeth*
1941	BRMSB publishes standards for model railways
1948	*Britain's railways nationalized as British Railways*
1950	BRMSB publishes revised standards for model railways
1953	Death of W.J. Bassett-Lowke
1956	Gauge O Guild founded
1964	*British Railways loses its 'way' – becoming British Rail*
1966	Tri-ang introduce Big Big trains
1967	Big Big concept sold to Lima, Italy
1968	*End of standard-gauge steam on British Rail*
1973	Lima introduces range of O-gauge train sets
1975	Metal Models GWR 'Siphon' kit
1979	Sevenscale L&Y 'Pug' kit wins Design Centre Award
1989	Gauge O Guild issue revised standards for O gauge
1990	Specialised Products releases RTR 'Jinty'
1993	85A Models all-plastic RTR 15in Hunslet
1995	Ace Trains founded by Allen Levy
1996	Ace Trains releases coarse-scale replica Hornby 4-4-4 tank; Bassett-Lowke acquired by Corgi
1997	First Bachmann Brass RTR Mk1 coaches released
2004	Skytrex RTR wagons introduced
2005	Heljan RTR 'Hymek'
2009	Lionheart RTR GWR 64xx pannier tank; last Bachmann Brassworks RTR loco – Ivatt 2MT 2-6-0
2012	Ixion RTR Hudswell Clarke 0-6-0ST
2013	San Cheng ends production of all-brass RTR
2015	RTR Dapol 'Terrier', Lionheart 'Mogul' and Minerva Models Peckett
2016	Gauge O Guild sixtieth anniversary; RTR Dapol 08 Diesel shunter; Heljan announce first RTR steam locomotive – GWR 61xx 2-6-2T – followed by GWR 43xx 'Mogul' and RTR Class 117/120 DMU, Class 121 and 128 railcars. Hatton's combine with Heljan to produce A3, A4 and Gresley teak stock.

The story of O gauge over the past sixty years has been one of gradual improvement and progress. It has taken a long time to shake off the image of unrealistic O-gauge tinplate toy trains and pre-war coarse-scale standards, or the belief that it is just a refuge of the dedicated scratch-builder, but as the Gauge O Guild celebrates its Diamond Jubilee, it is thanks to those early fine-scale pioneers and the support of some farsighted manufacturers that the foundations of an O-gauge renaissance were laid. Far from being a minority interest – as the promoters of a recent 'modern image' show described 7mm-scale modelling – the increased level of trade support including Peco's new O-gauge Setrack and the introduction of realistically priced small tank locomotives is attracting even more modellers into the senior scale. In the twenty-first century it is certainly one of the strongest and fastest growing parts of our hobby – we may well see O gauge once again become the first choice of railway modellers.

There are many model railway clubs and societies meeting around the country on a regular weekly or monthly basis. Many have an O-gauge section and can provide information and experience for those new to the hobby. Contact details, club news and details of events are published regularly in the popular model railway press. A number of specialist societies, the Gauge O Guild being foremost amongst these, also offer support, technical advice, area meetings, quarterly magazine and newsletter, as well as other useful services of interest to O-gauge modellers and collectors.

7mm Narrow Gauge Association
Modelling narrow-gauge railways in 7mm scale
www.7mmnga.org.uk

Arge Spur0 e.V.
O-gauge modelling in Germany
www.argespur0.de

Association of 16mm Narrow Gauge Modellers
Modelling narrow-gauge railways in 16mm scale
www.16mm.org.uk

Association of Larger Scale Railway Modellers
For modellers from S scale to large-scale live steam
www.alsrm.org.uk

Bassett-Lowke Society
For collectors of the products of Bassett-Lowke
www.bassettlowkesociety.org.uk

Broad Gauge Society
Modelling Brunel's broad gauge in all scales
www.broadgauge.org.uk

Cercle du Zéro
O-gauge modelling in France
www.cercleduzero.fr

DEMU (Diesel and Electric Modellers United)
Modelling the UK diesel and electric era in all scales
www.demu.org.uk

Gauge O Guild
Premier society for O gauge and 7mm scale
www.gauge0guild.com

HMRS (Historical Model Railway Society)
Promoting historical accuracy for modellers
www.hmrs.org.uk

Hornby Railway Collector's Association
For collectors of the products of Binns Road
www.hrca.net

Industrial Railway Society
Researches all aspects of industrial railways throughout the UK
www.irsociety.co.uk

Leeds Stedman Trust
Source of spares, repairs and technical advice for LMC enthusiasts
www.leedsstedmantrust.org

NMRA British Region
For modellers of American railroads
www.nmrabr.org.uk

Preston O Gauge Group
Monthly open days on group's O gauge Hawksbridge layout
www.prestonogauge.org.uk

Scale7 Group
Supports modellers working to true-to-scale 33mm gauge
www.scaleseven.org.uk

Spoor Nul Contact
O-gauge modelling in Holland
www.spoornul.nl

The Model Railway Club
The oldest model railway club in the world
www.themodelrailwayclub.org

Train Collectors Society
For those with a broad interest in collecting toy and model trains
www.traincollectors.org.uk

CHAPTER TWO

STANDARD, NARROW OR BROAD GAUGE?

GETTING ON THE RIGHT TRACK: MAKING SENSE OF SCALE AND GAUGE

It is reasonable to assume that the majority of modellers starting out in – or moving up to – O gauge will be modelling standard-gauge railways, that is with a prototype track gauge of 4ft 8½in (1,435mm). There will be a smaller proportion following narrow gauge – either 7mm scale using a variety of different track gauges, or to varying scales using 32mm-gauge track – whilst the least number (but there really ought to be

Full-size trackwork at Cheltenham Lansdown, c.1960, with Caprotti 'Black Five' 4-6-0 No.44742 arriving on a northbound train. After the regional boundary change and track alterations at Lansdown Junction in 1958, a Western Region tubular steel post bracket with upper quadrant arms has replaced the original LMS bracket signal on the opposite platform – a nightmare for modellers!

ROY TAYLOR/JOHN EMERSON COLLECTION

more of you!) will choose either Brunel's archaic but glorious 7ft 0¼in broad gauge, or 5ft 3in gauge as used, for example, in Ireland. For UK modellers of the standard gauge in 7mm (1:43.5) scale, the Gauge O Guild recognizes three basic standards today. These are:

- fine 32mm gauge (as used by RTR manufacturers)
- Scale7 33mm gauge (dead-scale track and wheel standards)
- coarse 32mm gauge (overscale flanges and wheel standards, incompatible with fine scale).

In America, modellers work to ¼in (1:48) scale, the majority of RTR standard-gauge equipment being produced to run on 32mm-gauge track, which equates to a scale 5ft track gauge. Proto48 standards were introduced for US modellers wishing to work to dead-scale standards. European O-gauge modellers work to 6.8mm (1:45) scale, giving the correct dimensions for standard-gauge track. The major scale/gauge combinations in general use for standard-gauge railways grouped under the umbrella term of O gauge are given in Table 3.

American outline O-scale locomotives and stock are produced to a slightly smaller scale than their 7mm-scale UK counterparts, but still appear large in comparison.

Table 3 Major O Gauge/Scales in General Use for Standard Gauge

Notation	Scale	Ratio	Track Gauge	Equates to	Definition
O	¼in	1:48	1¼in (32mm)	5ft	US O scale (NMRA standards)
Proto48	¼in	1:48	29.87mm	4ft 8½in	US O scale (dead scale)
O	6.8mm	1:45	32mm	4ft 8½in	European O gauge (MOROP standards)
O-MF	7mm	1:43.5	31.5mm	4ft 6in	UK O gauge (gauge/flangeways tightened)
O	7mm	1:43.5	32mm	4ft 7in	UK O gauge (fine scale)
S7	7mm	1:43.5	33mm	4ft 8½in	UK (dead scale)
Coarse	7mm	1:43.5	32mm	4ft 7in	coarse-scale standards

FINE SCALE: MAKING THE MOST OF RTR

O-gauge track has come a long way from the days of third-rail or 'stud' contact and overscale rail with cast-metal chairs that required pinning to massive wooden sleepers. These days, there are plenty of ready-to-use products that will provide a short cut when building a layout. Most O-gauge layouts seen at exhibitions or described in the pages of the model press will be fine scale – that is to say running on 32mm-gauge track – and this is the gauge typically used by most modellers moving into O gauge. Ready-to-use O-gauge track is much more accurate to track gauge than its 4mm OO counterpart, providing yet another advantage for moving up to O gauge! Although equating to a proto-type track gauge of 4ft 7in (1,397mm) (2.7 per cent inaccuracy), this is five times more accurate than the large discrepancy found in RTR OO gauge (13.2 per cent inaccuracy).

Probably the best known and most popular ready-to-use track system is Peco 'Streamline'. Produced in yard-long lengths in bullhead or flat-bottom rail section, it is readily available through many model shops, at shows or by mail order, enabling a layout to be built in a reasonable amount of time. A range of matching pointwork is also produced, including newly introduced points to match the flat-bottom track. Both track and points are robust enough to survive laying, lifting and relaying several times on successive layouts, or for a long life out in the garden. An additional advantage is that if you have used this type of track in a smaller scale, you will already be quite comfortable with its use for O gauge.

Fine-scale O gauge – 7mm scale with a track gauge of 32mm on the author's 'Gifford Street' layout. Points are handbuilt; plain track is Peco Streamline. Photographed some years ago, before the missing check rails in the crossover were finally added. TONY WRIGHT, COURTESY BRITISH RAILWAY MODELLING

Whilst it is probably true to say that the majority of O-gauge modellers are happy to use 'Streamline', it does have its detractors. Sleeper spacing and width is a compromise to suit both UK and overseas markets and the points do not entirely conform to how the prototype is constructed. Points, especially the curved variety that have an annoying straight section through the curve, may also need alteration to suit DCC operation. However, if care is taken over laying, painting and ballasting, very satisfactory results can be achieved – indeed, the majority of plain track on my 'Gifford Street' layout utilizes Peco 'Streamline' bullhead and flat-bottom track. For those wishing to build their own track and points, Peco also offers a

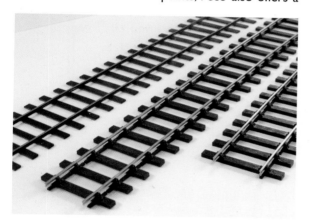

range of 'Individulay' components, including realistic concrete sleepers for flat-bottom track, especially useful for modellers of the British Railways period and into the Privatization era.

For the dedicated builder of track and pointwork, by far the largest range of track-building components is produced by C&L Finescale and is available from them by mail order, at shows or through selected stockists. For the modeller concerned with producing accurate scale track, all C&L components conform to prototype practice and track templates give relevant dimensions for track and siding spacing, as well as sleeper spacing, and sleeper widths for pre-Grouping and post-Grouping practice. Accurate ready-to-use plain track is also available in metre lengths, complemented by a wide range of components for building points and crossings to fine-scale O or Scale7 standards. Components are even available for building narrow- or broad-gauge baulk road.

Although some modellers may initially be put off at the thought of constructing their own track or pointwork, by using the various jigs, gauges and templates supplied by C&L as well as ready-assembled crossing vees and profiled switch blades, the task of assembly is made relatively easy. Complete kits for points, crossings and slip formations are also available 'off the shelf'. It is worth noting that C&L also sells Peco

ABOVE: *Three of the most popular O-gauge track systems – Marcway copper clad (left), C&L (centre), and Peco 'Streamline'.*

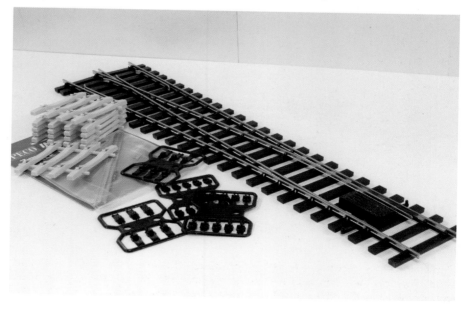

Peco 'Electrofrog' point and 'Individulay' components, including concrete sleepers, point blades and chairs for flat-bottom track and pointwork.

ABOVE: **Peco 'Streamline' pointwork was used to speed up track laying on the new permanent section of 'Gifford Street'. The late Peter Marshall looks on as the junction with the reversing loop is being laid in. On the right is the incline that would lead to the planned terminus station.**

Peco 'Streamline' track being laid on the extended 'Gifford Street' – cork tiles are used for the track bed and cosmetic sleepers will fill any awkward gaps after the rest of the tracklaying has been completed.

Take care if using track pins to lay track – always drill through the sleeper first and do not drive the pin in too hard or the sleeper may be deformed. Pin at the centre of sleepers, not at the sleeper ends, so as to avoid unnecessary kinks in straight track.

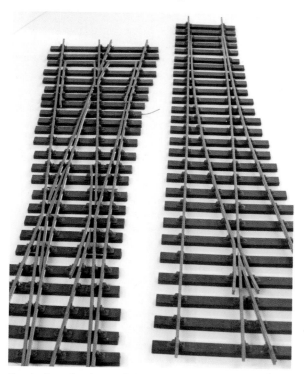

Examples of pointwork built up using components available from the extensive C&L range.

'Gifford Street' under construction in 2003. Plain track is Peco 'Streamline'; machined blades, stock rails and crossing vees are from Waverley point kits (sadly no longer available), with sleepers and chairs from the C&L range. Above baseboard point rodding was later replaced by Tortoise point machines installed below the baseboard. The stark white plastic trunking in the headshunt is the timberwork for the sand drag – rather shorter than the prototype but all that could be fitted in the space available.

track as well. Some modellers prefer to build their track using plywood sleepers with moulded plastic chairs glued to the sleeper. This results in a surprisingly robust track system – the chairs are effectively 'welded' into the grain of the sleeper by the solvent adhesive. The basic technique is to stain the sleepers before construction begins, chairs are then threaded on to the rail, one rail is glued in position and the other rail fixed in position using track gauges and straight edge to ensure proper alignment. Again, components are available from C&L, as well as other suppliers.

Alternatively, track can be constructed using copper-clad sleepers, with the rail soldered directly to the sleepers and cosmetic chairs added afterwards. Although the rail will not have that slightly raised off the sleeper effect of prototype track, careful ballasting can hide this. Components are available from

If you do not feel up to the task of building points and crossings, complex formations can either be custom-built to order, or are available ready made – like this scissors crossover from Marcway.

several suppliers, including C&L and Marcway in Sheffield. Marcway also offers a large range of ready-assembled solder-constructed plain track and points, including double junctions and scissors crossovers 'off the shelf'. The company will also build to order to your requirements and also provide useful 'half-track' – that is, solder-constructed track but with only one rail soldered in position for laying in curves or other special situations. The 'half-track is laid in position and the other rail soldered in place using track gauges to ensure correct alignment. Easy!

Recently there have been modellers who, dissatisfied with the relatively generous tolerances in 32mm-gauge pointwork but reluctant to convert to the dead-scale standards of Scale7, have taken to using a track gauge of 31.5mm. Referred to as O-MF, the use of this slightly reduced track gauge had certainly been suggested in the debate about fine- and coarse-scale O gauge as long ago as 1950 in the now defunct *Model Railway Constructor*. Put simply, although increasing the discrepancy in the track gauge to around 5 per cent, this has the effect of tightening up clearances through crossing vees and flangeways in an effort to promote better alignment and running qualities through points and crossings.

SCALE7: FOLLOWING THE PROTOTYPE

Those modellers not wishing to accept the compromise of fine-scale O gauge or O-MF can work to a set of dead-scale standards evolved by the Scale7 Society in the mid-1970s. The use of jigs, gauges and templates available through the Society or from specialist manufacturers makes the job of constructing track and points as easily as in fine scale. Although some locomotive kits now cater for S7 standards or include alternative frame stretchers and so on, most rolling stock (especially RTR) will need to be converted, most often by the simple expedient of replacing the wheel sets.

The Scale7 Society exists to promote the ideals of dead-scale modelling in 7mm and is supported by a growing number of manufacturers. Lionheart Models is one of the few manufacturers to offer the option of 'out of the box' RTR locomotives to S7 standards.

COARSE SCALE

The years between the two world wars tend to be seen as a golden age of coarse scale, thanks in part to the many TV programmes on antiques and collecting. These programmes have resulted in a growth of interest in old toy trains, drawing into the hobby many who would consider themselves to be primarily collectors, not modellers. At many exhibitions more often than not there is a larger crowd watching the action on the coarse-scale vintage tinplate layout than around some of the accurately modelled fine-scale layouts – which may say something to exhibition organizers, manufacturers and fine-scale modellers about what the paying visitor is really interested in!

However, collecting vintage tinplate can be a particularly expensive pastime and several firms have sprung up over recent years producing retro models in the style of the old tinplate trains, but at much more affordable prices. There has also been a growth in the 'semi-scale' model – accurate, detailed models but built to run on coarse-scale O-gauge track – and this is now firmly established as a small but dynamic branch of the hobby, increasingly, although somewhat confusingly, referred to as 'standard scale'. Ready-to-use retro-style two- and three-rail track is readily available and trade support and RTR models are provided by firms such as Ace Trains,

Tight curves and stiff gradients present a challenge for locomotives and drivers on Simon Thompson's impressive Scale7 'Aberbeeg' layout, seen at the STEAM museum in Swindon.

Coarse-scale Bassett-Lowke track – current collection is by 'spoon' collectors under the locomotive in contact with the raised third rail. Although there is plenty of original Bassett-Lowke around at reasonable prices, several firms now produce retro-style three-rail track.

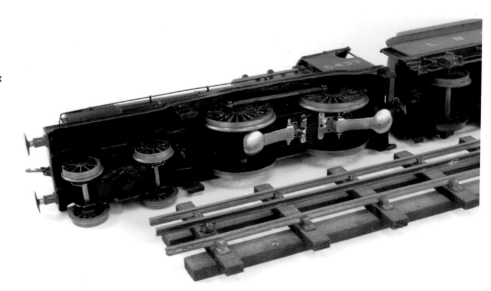

Darstaedt, W.J. Vintage and the Hornby-owned Bassett-Lowke brand, as well as many smaller cottage-style concerns. As with fine-scale modelling, there are a number of societies supporting collectors of Bassett-Lowke, Hornby, LMC and other vintage makes.

There is an increasing move these days to re-define coarse scale as 'standard scale', an historic term originally used to differentiate the 'coarse' track and wheel standards of the 1900s from the newly introduced fine-scale standards. Although a logical step at the time (coarse scale had been the accepted standard more or less since O gauge had been introduced), it is by no means the standard for the majority of O-gauge modellers today, especially those who seek accuracy and authenticity in the models and trackwork on their layouts. Whilst tinplate and retro-tinplate has a substantial following, as the term can be used in so many different contexts, it is confusing to say the least.

THE APPEAL OF NARROW GAUGE

So far, we have only considered standard-gauge railways. For most modellers railways with a gauge of less than 4ft 8½in (1,435mm) are commonly considered to be 'narrow gauge', although many main-line railways throughout the world run on track with a narrower gauge than the UK standard – 3ft 6in (1,067mm)-gauge railways in South Africa, for example. However, a better rule of thumb might be to consider any railway of 3ft (914mm) gauge or below as 'narrow gauge'. Interest in UK and overseas narrow gauge continues to grow and modellers choosing 7mm scale will find that one great advantage is that a realistic and fairly complex layout can be built in a modest amount of space.

7mm-scale narrow gauge used to great effect in an industrial setting on David Lenton's 'Staffordshire Pipe Works' layout. STEVE FLINT, COURTESY RAILWAY MODELLER

Continental narrow gauge can provide some attractive prototypes for the modeller. This is metre-gauge track and rolling stock from the Bemo Om range displayed at the Nuremburg Toy Fair. PETER MARRIOTT

The 7mm Narrow Gauge Association was formed in 1979 to 'promote and foster interest in narrow-gauge modelling in 7mm/ft and similar scales' and today members enjoy a wide range of kits, parts, accessories and RTR locomotives and rolling stock in a tangle of various scale/gauge combinations – although undoubtedly not deliberately designed to confuse! The most popular and commonly used are shown in Table 4.

Although outside the province of this book, it should be mentioned that the 32mm track gauge is utilized in New Zealand to model 3ft 6in (1,067mm)-gauge railways in 9mm scale, and also by 16mm-scale narrow-gauge modellers to give a dead-scale equivalent of 2ft (610mm) gauge (1:19.05 scale) – see the website of the Association of 16mm Narrow Gauge Modellers for further details.

Table 4   Major Scales/Gauges in General Use for Narrow Gauge

7mm scale (1:43.5)

Notation	Track Gauge	Equates to	Definition
O21	21mm	3ft	Irish and Isle of Man prototypes
–	18mm	2ft 6in	
O16.5	16.5mm	2ft 4in	Talyllyn, Corris, Welshpool & Llanfair
O14	14mm	2ft	Ffestiniog, Welsh Highland, quarry tramways
On12	12mm	21in	
On18	9mm	18in	
O9/On15	9mm	15in	Ravenglass & Eskdale, Romney, Hythe & Dymchurch
On6.5	6.5mm	10½in	Fairbourne Railway as running today

7mm scale (1:45)

Notation	Track Gauge	Equates to	Definition
Om	22.2mm	1,000mm	metre-gauge prototypes
Oe	16.5mm	750mm (2ft 5½in)	
Op	9mm	15¾in (400mm)	

¼in scale (1:48)

Notation	Track Gauge	Equates to	Definition
On42	22.2mm	3ft 6in	
On3	19mm	3ft	
On2	12.7mm	2ft	US dead-scale equivalent of O14
On30/On2 1/2	16.5mm	2ft 6in	US logging railroads between 2 and 3ft gauge
Of	9mm	450mm	

Bachmann's On30 Shay-geared locomotive has become a popular choice for ¼in scale layouts based on American narrow-gauge logging lines and using commercially available 16.5mm-gauge track.
TONY WRIGHT, COURTESY BRITISH RAILWAY MODELLING

THE BROAD APPROACH

Conversely, any railway with a gauge greater than the 'standard' 4ft 8½in (1,435mm) is said to be 'broad gauge', the most well-known being Brunel's ill-fated 7ft 0¼in broad gauge adopted by the Great Western Railway from 1838 to abolition in 1892. The Broad Gauge Society exists to cater specifically for the needs of modellers in all scales of this historic episode in our railway history. A growing range of kits and components is now available to encourage the broad-gauge modeller. The BG7 standard enables 7mm modellers to model the broad gauge to dead-scale dimensions (Scale7 standards).

Often suggested, although I have to admit to never having seen any actual models, is to use standard 32mm gauge with a scale of ¼in to the foot (1:48) to represent Irish 5ft 3in (1,600mm) gauge. Unfortunately, there are several practical problems in adopting this approach, specifically that 7mm-scale wheel sets will not necessarily scale down to correct prototype sizes for ¼in scale, or will have far too many spokes, meaning that this remains a true scratch-builder's scale. Happily, however, there are several manufacturers providing 7mm-scale kits of Irish prototypes for modellers who will either run them on standard 32mm gauge or build their own track to the correct gauge.

Brunel's ill-fated 7ft broad gauge makes a fascinating and unusual historical subject for a 7mm-scale layout. In this scene on Graham Powell's 'Gatcombe' layout a 'Leo' Class 2-4-0 saddle tank heads a short coal train. The 'Leo' Class saddle tanks were rebuilds dating from 1874.

STEVE FLINT, COURTESY RAILWAY MODELLER

Broad-gauge beauty – a 7mm-scale model of Great Southern & Western Railway of Ireland 3-cylinder 800 Class 4-6-0 No.802 Tailté. Scratch-built by an unknown Irish builder to run on 36.75mm-gauge track and with working inside motion, it was acquired some years ago at auction along with a 400 Class 4-6-0 and GNR(I) S Class 4-4-0 No.174 Carrantuohill.

Table 5 Broad Gauge

Notation	Ratio	Scale	Track Gauge	Actual	Prototypes
–	¼in	1:48	32mm	5ft	Irish broad gauge
–	7mm	1:43.5	36.75mm	5ft 3in	Irish broad gauge
R7	7mm	1:43.5	48mm	–	UK broad gauge (now defunct)
O7	7mm	1:43.5	49mm	7ft	UK broad gauge
BG7	7mm	1:43.5	49.2mm	7ft 0¼in	UK broad gauge (S7 standards)

Small tank locos, sharp curves and lots of beer! A brewery complex would make a good subject for a small layout – more than 25 miles of private sidings linked the various breweries at Burton upon Trent with the BR network.
TRANSPORT AGE/JOHN EMERSON COLLECTION

IDEAL FOR INDUSTRY

For the modeller really strapped for space, Peco has recently introduced an innovative range of O-gauge 'Setrack'. Peco, being a relatively conservative company not known for throwing money at loss-making ideas, obviously sees the potential growth of smaller O-gauge layouts, understandable with the number of small O-gauge locomotives being produced or under development at the moment. This new track system is supplied as a box of eight curved sections of 40½in (1,020mm) radius to make a complete circle of track, plus a box of eight straight sections each measuring 15½in (400mm) long, so will enable some fairly compact tight-radius layouts to be developed.

At the time of writing, left- and right-hand points were shortly to be introduced. Most usefully, this new 'Setrack' system is fully compatible with the existing range of Peco 'Streamline' track and is ideal for creating the type of small shunting yard, industrial or dock-side layout that once abounded with sharp curves and small tank locos, providing an exceptionally good entrance point for the novice modeller. Other sectional track systems are also available, mainly produced by overseas manufacturers such as Atlas, Lionel and so on.

Finally, if after reading through this section you decide you are completely ham-fisted, have two left thumbs, or could not possibly lay even sectional track, then don't worry – there are specialist firms around who will build track for you, lay it and wire it, or even build a complete layout for you. Examples are Norman Solomons of Quantock Models or Borg-Rail. So one way or another everyone can aspire to having an O-gauge layout!

THE END OF THE LINE

Have another look at the many different ways that sidings end. Buffer stops (more correctly stop blocks) are available ready-assembled or as kits, but can easily be 'distressed' to represent the result of a heavy shunt. Not all are painted red; in some areas white is the colour most often used. A sleeper across the rails with red flag and/or lamp provides a temporary stop block. Do not forget end loading bays where a hefty timber baulk provides protection for the platform end, or in some instances the stop block is built into the brickwork.

SUPPLIERS OF TRACK AND TRACKLAYING SERVICES

Atlas
Two- and three-rail tinplate style track
Available in the UK from Gaugemaster
Tel: 01903 884488
www.gaugemaster.com

Borg-rail
Custom-built trackwork
www.borg-rail.co.uk

C&L Finescale Modelling Ltd
Track-building components and kits, laser-cut building kits, solders and fluxes
Tel: 01179 505470
www.finescale.org.uk

Lionel
A good match for Hornby tinplate track
Available in the UK from Tennents Trains
Tel: 0121 550 1266
www.tennentstrainsofhalesowen.co.uk

Maldon Rail Centre
Replica three-rail O-gauge track
Tel: 01245 425413
www.maldonrail.com

Marcway
Ready-to-lay track and points, track and point kits, trackwork commissions
Shop: 0114 2449170
Technical or quotes: 01709 542951
www.smpscaleway.com

Peco (Pritchard Patent Product Co. Ltd)
Standard- and narrow-gauge track, points, Setrack, lineside buildings and accessory kits, distributed lines
Tel: 01297 21542
www.peco-uk.com

Quantock Models (Norman Solomon)
Custom trackwork
www.quantockmodels.co.uk

W.J.Vintage
Merkur three-rail tinplate track
Tel: 07711 092497
www.wjvintage.co.uk

CHAPTER THREE

MAKING A START

Model railways can provide a richly satisfying and creative hobby for a lifetime, although it can be difficult and frustrating to get started. Moving up to O gauge from the smaller scales can be a daunting prospect. Often there may be a considerable collection of smaller-scale models built up over a number of years and a reluctance to get rid of them for a variety of reasons, not least of which may be sentimental value. There may also be a layout to dispose of. Preconceived ideas or misconceptions about 7mm and O gauge can also get in the way, ranging from 'lack of space', 'it's too expensive', or 'I don't have the time', to 'I haven't got the necessary skills'.

IF YOU MODEL IN OO OR N – YOU CAN MODEL IN O!

One of the first things to learn is that it is not at all necessary to be a highly skilled modeller to produce a half-decent layout – in any scale. It is all too easy

Tracklaying in progress on the permanent section of 'Gifford Street' using Peco 'Streamline' track and points. Time spent in careful planning before tracklaying can prevent costly alterations later.

Ready-to-run O-gauge stock is now available to a standard previously only enjoyed in the smaller scales. An Ixion Hudswell Clarke 0-6-0ST hauls a train of Lionheart open wagons on 'Gifford Street' – all modern high-quality RTR stock that will run straight 'out of the box', enabling you quickly to get something up and running.

to be discouraged by the 'armchair modeller', who may tell you that it is necessary to build all of your stock and track from scratch in order to be any kind of modeller, or that only kit or scratch-built locomotives and rolling stock make acceptable scale models. This, of course, is sheer nonsense. These days there is an increasing amount of sophisticated RTR O-gauge equipment that can be bought off the shelf to enable the beginner or novice modeller to get something up and running in far less time than it takes to build everything from scratch or from kits. It is not only the novice who can take advantage of RTR models – unfortunately the time factor will become increasingly important with advancing age. But you can save that valuable commodity by initially stocking the layout quickly with RTR, effectively 'buying time' in which you can then build all of that stock you *really* need at your leisure.

GET SOMETHING RUNNING

This is not to detract from the added pleasures that building from scratch or from kits can bring to the hobby. It is just that in the initial stages of getting to grips with building a layout the beginner or novice may

be well advised to consider what is readily available off the shelf. By all means, buy a kit or two to construct, but the fundamental rule is to *get something running*. Fail to do so and you run the risk of a gradual loss of interest, then your project may eventually stall or fall by the wayside. There are also subtle barriers that modellers can erect to prevent layouts being built. Given the necessary resources, the unwary modeller may be tempted to buy all the kits and equipment required for that dream project, but is then unable to complete the dream when confronted with a mountain of locomotives and stock to build – 'I'll build the layout once I've finished building all the stock' is really a case of putting the proverbial cart before the horse. It will come as no surprise that if you are turning threescore years and ten and still have a hundred wagon kits, thirty-five locomotive kits and goodness knows how many coach kits to build, you are very unlikely to see them running on your layout – that is, if you've actually got time to build it!

'But I could never achieve what you do' is another frequently heard comment at shows. The skills and techniques needed to model in O gauge are no different to those necessary to work in OO, 3mm scale, or N gauge – or any other modelling discipline, for that

Building kits can be an absorbing and enjoyable part of creating an O-gauge layout – this is a BR Banana Van from the Just Like The Real Thing range that features easy plug-together assembly for most parts – just add glue!

matter. In fact, it is often easier to model in the larger scale due to its greater size, and the fact that models are easier to handle. Every modeller has to start somewhere and all will have had their 'bad model' days, even the top names in the hobby – although they may not wish to admit it. But essentially if you can pick up a paintbrush, you can model in O gauge. If you have had experience of building a plastic kit, you can certainly model in O gauge. And if you have had an N-gauge or OO-gauge train set and nailed track to a board, then you can definitely model in O gauge; it is just a bit bigger, that's all. Even if you have no modelling experience, have never owned a train set, or have not taken any interest in model railways, at least have a go – you may surprise yourself and discover hidden talents, as well as immersing yourself in an immensely enjoyable and creative hobby.

THE RULE OF THREE: SPACE, TIME AND COST

It is important to get something running, even if it is a yard or two of track, the smallest of locomotives and a coach or wagon or two. Most aspiring modellers will at least have the room somewhere for a small layout and this can provide a useful learning curve and valuable experience in laying track, wiring, scenic development and, very importantly – troubleshooting. When things go wrong on a small layout they are invariably quite easy to fix, but problems on a large layout can be a serious headache – I speak from experience! Think of a small layout as a 'testbed' or stepping stone towards that dream layout. It will enable you to try out ideas and techniques, but can always be dismantled and recycled into the next layout or sold to provide funds towards a larger project as and when circumstances permit, then you can confidently put your new-found skills and experience to good use. However, it is important to remember that no layout is ever *really* complete – that would spoil the fun!

However, before planning your dream layout, buying or making baseboards, laying track or starting to build models, you need to ask yourself the following questions:

- First, do I have *space* for a layout?
- If I have the space, then what can I realistically *afford* to spend on my hobby?
- How much *spare time* will I have in which to build it?

These are not just key questions for the O-gauge modeller; modellers in all scales and gauges will face the same set of issues. If you are lucky enough to have a large room, attic or barn, do not fall into the trap of thinking that building a huge dream layout is an ideal solution. Having too much space on hand can be just as bad as having too little. The more space you have, the more time it will take to build and the more it will cost. Conversely, a layout built in a smaller space will take less time, can be detailed to a higher standard and cost less. Alternatively, buying everything RTR or ready-built can save time, but will increase costs. Balancing the time factor against space and cost can be thought of as a triangle, with space at the top, then cost and time at the bottom.

SPACE – NOT QUITE THE FINAL FRONTIER

Undoubtedly the most critical question is the perennial one of where to find space for a layout and your modelling activities, remembering that for much of the time a layout may not actually be in use and will probably considered an 'eyesore' (or worse) by the domestic authorities. The ultimate goal for most modellers is to find a convenient space equipped with light, heat and power where the layout can be installed permanently, or at least left for long periods without fear of damage or interference from other household or family activities. If you are moving up from one of the smaller scales, the domestic authorities may already have granted possession of a suitable location for a previous layout. But with the size of the average modern house having decreased over the years and many older houses divided into smaller living areas, not to mention a bedroom tax on certain parts of the community, finding a site for your layout can pose real problems. Obviously it is no good planning an ambitious main-line scheme if you are not likely to have the room to build it and if you really do not have anywhere to put a layout it may be pointless asking the other questions! However, there are usually a fair number of options to consider as suitable sites, especially for portable layouts.

A spare room can provide a fine location and has the added advantage of not being isolated from the rest of the family while you indulge your hobby. A permanent layout can be set up, with purpose-built storage or cupboards under to store stock, tools, books and magazines. If the room has shared usage (for example, a spare bedroom), it may be worth building a shelf around the room on which to put the layout. Alternatively, a portable line could be constructed and dismantled for storage when the room is required for other purposes.

Garden sheds might not be an obvious first choice for a layout, but can be turned into a cosy home once power, lighting and insulation have been installed, although you are not likely to get an O-gauge layout in anything less than a 10 × 8ft (3 × 2.5m) shed and even that will be on the small side. Remember that the internal dimensions will be less after allowing for framing, insulation and so on. An alternative is to have a custom-built shed erected and there are plenty of companies that will provide wooden structures to your specification, some even being built in a sympathetic railway-company style.

Garages are often thought of as natural sites for layouts, but will probably not provide a suitable location if the garage is not integral with the house, or not built of brick, block or concrete construction with a proper pitched roof. Even then, there can be a few problems to overcome – concrete floors create a lot of dust, so need to be levelled and sealed, while up and over doors are definitely not draught-proof and will let in dust, leaves and most of the local insect population, as well as mice and the odd toad or hedgehog. If there is another access door into the garage, it is better to use that and seal up the main doors. Whilst the garage may have light and power installed, this could mean that there are also household appliances to contend with – fridges, freezers or stacked washing machines and tumble driers may block the proposed 'right of way' and need resiting.

Depending on their condition, wooden garages can be treated like garden sheds with insulation, power, light and heating installed, but garages (and sheds) of metal construction, or clad in asbestos-type materials should be avoided. Concrete sectional garages with metal doors and corrugated roofing are also best avoided as potential sites for layouts. Many

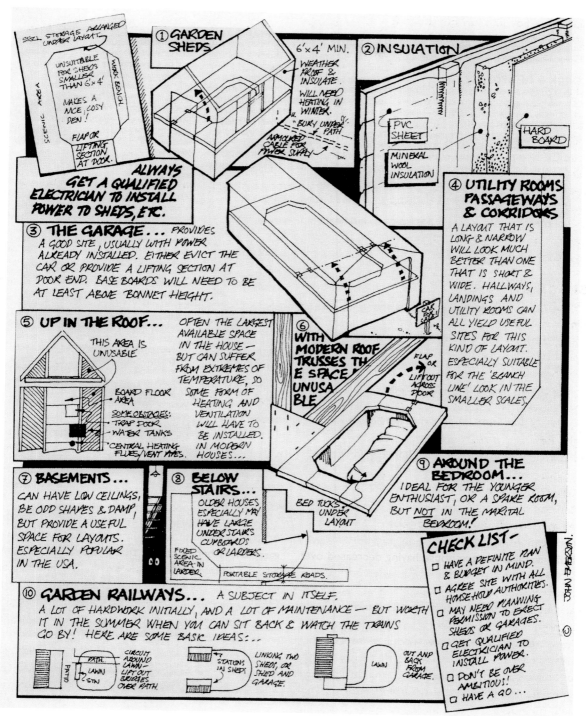

Finding a location where you can build your layout can be difficult – although not a comprehensive guide, these suggestions may inspire you to find the space in your home. Always seek professional advice before undertaking any major alterations and always use a qualified electrician to install power to sheds and garages and so on.

The garage can provide an ideal home for a self-contained railway, or as part of a garden line – this is the scene at 'Wallsea Main' on Barrie Walls' extensive O-gauge system.

excellent layouts have been built in sheds and garages, or linked via a garden line. However, it hardly needs emphasizing that mains electricity and the outdoors can be a lethal mix, so ensure that all mains wiring is carried out by a competent and qualified professional electrician.

The loft, attic, or roof space of older houses should not present too much of a problem as a potential site for a layout, but modern load-bearing roof trusses will get in the way and should on no account be altered without first seeking suitable professional advice from an experienced builder or structural engineer. Water tanks, cisterns and overflow pipes can also be inconveniently sited. A suitable means of access such as a properly installed loft ladder will have to be provided, power and lighting installed, and joists

boarded over to provide a floor to walk on. If significant alterations have to be carried out, these may need clearing with the appropriate planning department before any work is undertaken. Modern planning regulations may also restrict what you can do with the roof space – I know of at least one large layout where the owner has to contend with bats, a protected species!

As the roof void can get very hot in summer and extremely cold in winter, some form of insulation and ventilation will need to be considered. Remember also that not all of the roof area can be utilized due to the pitch of the roof limiting headroom under the eaves, but as this is probably the largest single space in the house, it is certainly worth considering. The roof space is more suited to permanent layouts than

The late George Hinchciffe at the controls of his O-gauge layout built in the roof space – bubble wrap around the roof timbers and suitable headgear helped to prevent bumps and bruises! PETER MARRIOTT

portable ones due to the problems of manhandling baseboards out through the access hatch.

A basement or cellar can also provide an excellent site for a layout, although damp and restricted headroom may pose a problem. While damp can usually be eradicated, the problem of low headroom will not go away. Flooring, lighting, power, heating and insulation may all need to be installed. As with layouts in the roof, it may prove awkward to move portable layouts on and off site. Most basements will have a decent floor surface, but cellars will often need a suitable floor laid. Finally, what about below stairs? Although not so common in houses these days, a large understairs cupboard or pantry could provide a useful home for part of an 'L'-shaped layout, with a portable section erected in the hall or passageway for operating sessions. Power and lighting may need to be installed, but avoid extension cables for providing power as these are only too easy to trip over.

If you definitely do not have room for a layout, how about a small diorama on which to display your models? Alternatively, join one of the Gauge O Guild area groups, or a local model railway club with an O-gauge contingent where you can run your locos and stock, or blag running rights on friend's layouts. It is also worth keeping in mind that, dependent upon age, most modellers will usually get round to building more than one layout in their lifetime. So a good idea, as already mentioned, is to start in a small way with a compact layout, begin to build up that impressive fleet of locos and rolling stock, then gradually move on to larger and more ambitious schemes as time and finances allow.

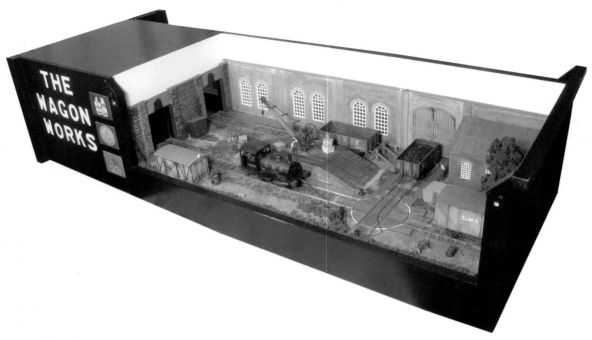

About as small as you can get in O-gauge – 'Wagon Works' is a working diorama built and exhibited at shows by Colin French. PAUL BASON, COURTESY RAILWAY MODELLER

While garden layouts are really outside the scope of this book, if you still cannot find a home for a layout there is always the garden to consider. In summer, there is nothing better than sitting outside enjoying a cool drink as you watch the trains go by. A framework will need to be erected for the tracks to be laid on, which can be of weather-proofed wood, bricks or blocks, or concrete. Plastic drainage pipes have also been used as supports for outdoor lines. Once erected, the framework can be disguised by judicious planting of shrubs and plants and can make a very attractive and unusual feature. Bridges, viaducts and other civil engineering features can also be incorporated, although you will have to ensure that any structures left out in the garden are completely weather-proof.

Most garden layouts either run out of and back into, or through a shed or garage, which is usually where control panels are situated. A garden scheme of this nature can be a satisfying project for a small group to build and run in a prototypical fashion. Some builders of garden lines arrange for covers to

be put over the tracks to protect them in the winter months, while others are happy to leave the tracks exposed all year round. Modern plastic-based track and pointwork is ideal for electrically powered lines in an outdoor environment, although you will have to take care if running live steam. Other options include semi-portable garden layouts built on removable baseboards that are taken indoors during bad weather and the winter months.

While each location mentioned above has its own advantages, it also raises its own particular set of problems. The garage, shed and roof space in particular can provide ideal accommodation, but remember that you may then be isolated from the rest of the family when engrossed in your hobby, something it is well to consider to avoid the possibility of family disputes. To help keep things tidy, permanent layouts can be set up with purpose-built storage units or cupboards underneath for the neat storage of stock, tools, books or magazines.

One other consideration with all these potential sites is security. Ensure that sheds, garages and

Members of the 'Loggies' (Luton MRC Gauge O Group) enjoy a running session on 'Gifford Street' – club layouts can provide an ideal opportunity to run your latest models if you do not have room for a layout.

*LEFT: **What could be better than watching trains in the garden on a summer's day? Barrie Walls enjoys the scene on the garden section of his 'Wallsea' layout.***

access to railway rooms can be securely locked and that stock and collections of models are kept well out of sight, as well as insured. It is wise not to advertise your interests to the outside world in general by displaying cast-iron signs, signals, or other railwayana where they can easily be seen from the road, spotted on online maps, or by satellite imagery or the increasing use of miniature camera-carrying drones.

COST: BUDGET FOR WHAT YOU *CAN* AFFORD

'But it is too expensive!' Some modellers seem to assume that because model railways are 'just a hobby', it should not cost a lot of money to indulge in. 'What's the best price you can do that for?' is the well-rehearsed question asked of traders at shows. Although we all like to find a bargain, remember that

A lengthy mineral train crosses Digswell (Welwyn) Viaduct out in the garden on Barrie Walls' O-gauge 'Wallsea' layout.

traders have to make a living too – and you may not always get the answer you were hoping for! Take up almost any other hobby, sport or pastime – golf, horse riding, shooting, restoring locomotives – and you will soon realize that O-gauge model railways are amongst the cheaper options. More seriously, and as with most things in life, you need to budget accordingly. As Cyril Freezer once remarked, 'as with any other hobby, your model railway is going to cost you just as much as you can afford to spend upon it'.

It is not necessary to own a large or elaborate system; after all, most modellers can only cope with operating one train at a time – even with DCC – and a small or modest layout can have a lot going for it in terms of space, the time required to build it and the amount of stock ultimately required to run it. In other words, if you do not have space for a large layout, it is pretty pointless setting out to build or buy a fleet of 'Pacifics'. And although you may have somewhere else to run them, what about the trains they will pull? Small layouts are also easier to transport to and from exhibitions and require much less maintenance than larger, more complex schemes. A further satisfying point about small layouts is that they can be detailed to a high standard more easily and far more quickly than a large O-gauge empire.

Building baseboards at the start of a project is usually the period when a lot of expenditure occurs in a fairly short space of time, but after this initial build, remaining costs can be spread over a much longer period of time. Importantly, remember when budgeting that in addition to all those lovely locomotives and stock, you will need to purchase materials (timber, plywood, MDF and so on), as well as consumables (screws, glue, knife blades and the like), track and points, wire, controllers, switches and scenic materials. This can amount to a considerable sum for larger projects. It is also worth bearing in mind that unlike some other hobbies, once the layout is built it should have a residual value.

TIME: GIVE YOURSELF A TIME BUDGET

Layout building is a notorious consumer of time and as 'Parkinson's Law' predicts, work expands to fill whatever time is available. Modern life can also impose many conflicting demands on time, but have you actually thought about how you spend your free time? For instance, do you really need to spend hours

Having a large amount of space at your disposal can create just as many problems as not having enough space. A suspended ceiling had to be built, electrics rerouted and new daylight-balanced fluorescent lighting installed in the barn before it could become a permanent home for 'Gifford Street'.

on the computer, social media or slumped in front of the TV? Give yourself a time budget. Miss out on the pub one night, get up an hour earlier, take something to work to build in your lunch hour or in front of the TV. There are many creative ways in which you can acquire extra valuable modelling time.

If you are working all day and have a family to run in the evenings and at weekends, there will not be much of this precious commodity left to spend on building your layout. Put simply, try to tailor your project to fit in with the amount of free time you have at your disposal, or you may never finish it. Then disillusionment may set in and any further interest in the hobby may be lost. Remember, too, that models and layouts are not going to be built overnight, so work out a long-term time budget for your layout. Think in

terms of small steps, not big leaps, and be prepared to measure your project in months or years, but a budget will give you something to measure actual progress against.

PLANNING A LAYOUT

There are two types of layout – *fixed* and *portable*. The fixed layout, as its name implies, is one that is built into its surroundings so that it is not portable. If it becomes necessary to be moved (often due to a house move), it usually results in its partial or complete destruction. Many large and 'last great project' layouts tend to be of the fixed type.

On the other hand, portable layouts are designed to be transportable. Portable layouts fall into two categories. First is the *exhibition* layout, designed to be built on a series of robust baseboards that can easily be transported to an exhibition venue where they can be erected and locked together mechanically and electrically, enabling the layout to function as it would when at home. Larger layouts of this type tend to be club or group projects, while smaller layouts may be privately owned or built by clubs and groups.

The second type of portable layout is also built on a series of baseboards, although not designed to be as easily transportable as the exhibition type. In fact, it may never leave the owner's home, except due to a house move or other exceptional event. The reason for this semi-portability is twofold. In the event of a move, not only will there not be the destruction associated with trying to move a fixed layout, but it should also be a relatively easy task to fit into its new

home. Unfortunately, this is also the Achilles heel of this type of layout. Invariably the new location will bear little resemblance to the original home and a lot of heartbreaking and destructive rebuilding ensues until the owner eventually decides to cut his or her losses, break the layout up and start all over again!

Layout plans, whether fixed or portable, can be categorized as three types – continuous circuit, end-to-end, or out and back, and it is these – or variations and combinations of these – upon which all model railway layouts are based. Most modellers will be familiar with the popular train set in the smaller scales, which usually enables a train to run round a small continuous circuit of track. Points, sidings and stations can be added to make the circuit more complex and to give purpose to the train's journey. Although the pundits may well try to deny it, many large layouts

Staging for the fixed layout under construction in the barn – the white conduit carries 240V AC mains power safely out of harm's way and feeds twin 13A sockets fixed at a convenient height to the baseboard facia.

seen at exhibitions are simply variations of the continuous train-set circuit, although on a grand scale, the most common variation being to add storage sidings to one side, usually opposite the station area. In many cases these are arranged to be hidden from public view, in which case they are referred to as hidden sidings, with the tracks from the rest of the scenically treated layout passing through a back scene, most often by means of a tunnel or road overbridge, a device known as a scenic divide or scenic break.

Besides storing stock not in use on the layout, storage sidings also serve another useful function, as they can be thought of as representing the rest of the British railway system. Trains can then be run from your own particular station on the layout to London, Plymouth, Edinburgh, or whatever destination takes your fancy, all represented in the imagination by the storage roads. This can also open up the possibility of

scheduling trains in a more realistic manner, or working to a timetable.

A further variation on the continuous layout theme is to arrange the straight tracks on one side of the circuit to parallel the tracks on the other side to produce a dumb-bell. Alternatively, the tracks can be joined together with points at either end of the 'bells' to form two return loops for a single-track layout, although this will also produce added complications in the wiring. To allow a greater number of trains to run, several storage loops can be added to the dumb-bells. This can often form the basis for outdoor lines in the garden where a suitable shed can house a station, goods yard and storage area for locomotives and stock in bad weather.

The end-to-end or point-to-point layout has become increasingly popular, as it can be fitted into a relatively compact area and when coupled with a

Fiddle yards or storage sidings are not just used to store rolling stock – they can also represent the rest of the railway system.

suitable set of storage sidings to represent the rest of the rail system (usually referred to as a fiddle yard on point-to-point systems), working trains in a pro- totypical manner to a timetable or schedule becomes achievable and can be most absorbing. Small end-to- end lines lend themselves to locations such as goods yards, lineside industries, military railways or dock- yards and so on, that require regular shunting and this can also provide endless hours of enjoyment. A relatively modern development is the minimal micro- layout, which takes the elements of a yard or small station built into as small a space as possible. On this small scale its increased popularity is due to the high operational interest that it can provide.

Given enough space, there is no reason why an end-to-end layout need be small, though. Arranged around three sides of a garden, for instance, would provide a reasonably long run in O gauge and might also accommodate more than one station, allowing for an intensive suburban service to be operated with tank engines and non-corridor stock, or electric or DMUs. There is no reason why the line could not feature terminus-to-terminus running, instead of the usual set of storage sidings at one or both ends, as on Barrie Walls' O-gauge layout 'Wallsea'. Furthermore, by modelling one station as, say, LNER, and the other BR 'Modern Image', the line could be run with two sets of stock in two distinct historical periods, giving twice as much variety. The LNER operating session would use the BR station as a fiddle yard, while the reverse would happen during BR running sessions.

This idea could be taken a stage further at exhi- bitions by linking two end-to-end layouts together and running through-trains between them, a practice that seems to have fallen out of favour these days, possibly due to increasing interest in modular lay-

Trains are worked from fiddle yard to fiddle yard through the station on the scenic section of 'Brindleby Walk', a portable O-gauge layout from the Spalding MRC.

outs. With this US-inspired system, individual base-boards are built by a number of different modellers, then brought together at shows, or closed running sessions. The key to the success of a modular lay-out is that everyone works to a standardized set of dimensions and recommended practices, so as to enable tracks and wiring to fit together regardless of what is on the next module. While this will ide-ally work with single-track modules, introducing a

second or multiple tracks (a main line or shunting yards, for example) means working to exacting tol-erances to avoid any potential mismatch of tracks. Standards for modular layouts have been published by the NMRA.

Another American idea that has not yet found a great deal of favour in the UK is the idea of the mul-tilevel or 'stacked' layout. This can either take the form of a single layout that loops round on itself, or

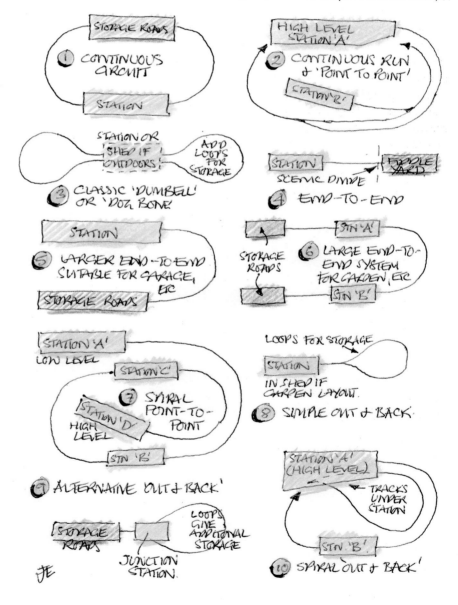

Most layouts are variations on a continuous circuit, or a form of end-to-end. The majority of large O-gauge exhibition layouts are based on the continuous circuit – even 'Gifford Street' is just a larger development of the basic train set!

two entirely separate layouts, one above the other, but both fully scenic, unlike layouts where a lower level is used purely for hidden storage roads. This could be useful for small layouts, using a proprietary shelf bracket system to support the baseboards, and also where the owner is interested in, say, pre-Grouping and the post-Privatization railway and can indulge in both periods without them clashing. In all cases it will be more than likely that some form of lighting will need to be installed for the lower level.

A further variation on the point-to-point system is to run from fiddle yard to fiddle yard with through stations. In some respects this can offer the best of all worlds as services can be run from station to station, yard to station, or with the 'off-stage' fiddle yards representing the rest of the railway system, non-stop through expresses can be run from 'London' (Yard 'A') to 'Manchester' (Yard 'B') or any other destination you may fancy. Where plenty of space is available, or in smaller areas when using narrow gauge, a further variation of the point-to-point system is the spiral, favoured by American modellers. This can either be arranged so that the tracks climb and cross over each other, or, given enough space, with walkways following the tracks, allowing operators to follow trains around to a limited degree.

Finally, we come to the out and back type of layout. Again, these will need a lot of space to accommodate the return loop, but can form the basis of an interesting garden scheme, with the terminus in a garden shed or garage. With the addition of storage roads on the loops, trains can be held until required to return to the station, avoiding an unrealistic out and back journey and effectively appearing to have gone to a destination before returning.

These, then, are the main different types of basic layout that will be encountered and for the most part all published layout plans will be permutations of these.

BASEBOARDS

All layouts need a baseboard of some sort to provide a stable surface on which the track can be laid. There are several methods of achieving this, usually referred to as solid top, open top and 'L'-girder. At its simplest, a solid-top baseboard can be a piece of sheet material screwed to a supporting framework. Traditionally, this has taken the form of $\frac{1}{2}$in chipboard and 2 × 1in (50 × 25mm) softwood. This is by no means ideal, but has the benefit of being relatively easy to assemble from materials readily available at the local timber merchant or DIY store. Unfortunately, chipboard is not only heavy, but also unstable when damp and difficult to pin track to, so, along with MDF and blockboard, is best avoided as a baseboard surface. On no account should hardboard be used, as it is not only too thin, but the surface is also much too hard.

Recommended best practice these days is to use plywood. Although more expensive, best-quality birch ply is considered the most appropriate material for the needs of the railway modeller. Cheaper grades of plywood should be avoided, as they are not as stable so are more prone to warping, not so strong at the edges so may split and splinter, and may have annoying voids so need greater care taken to get a good finish. Unnecessary weight can be eliminated by building the entire baseboard from plywood. For those who either do not have the time to build their own baseboards, or lack the confidence to attempt construction, self-assembly baseboard kits are available in a range of sizes from a variety of commercial sources. For those wishing to build their own, many timber merchants and DIY stores will cut the material to size for an additional charge. However, even when cut on a large bed-saw, beware of plywood sheets moving during the cut, producing a 'banana'-shaped baseboard member that will be virtually impossible to use. Laser-cut baseboard kits and components are increasingly being produced and this may offer the better solution for absolute accuracy, although at higher initial cost.

The photograph illustrates a typical baseboard kit, kindly supplied by Model Railway Solutions, which builds into a 4 × 2ft (1,219 × 610mm) baseboard. The kits are supplied in flat-pack form, complete with screws, glue and full instructions, and are easily assembled on a convenient flat surface. The frames illustrated were built on a large kitchen table and assembled at a sedate pace within an hour. Once assembled, the completed frames were left overnight for the glue to

The principle of 'L'-girder construction for fixed layouts – the thickness of material used will depend on the size of the proposed layout, but larger-section timber will enable the 'L'-girders to span greater width with fewer supporting legs. Cross members can be trimmed back after construction and a facia added.

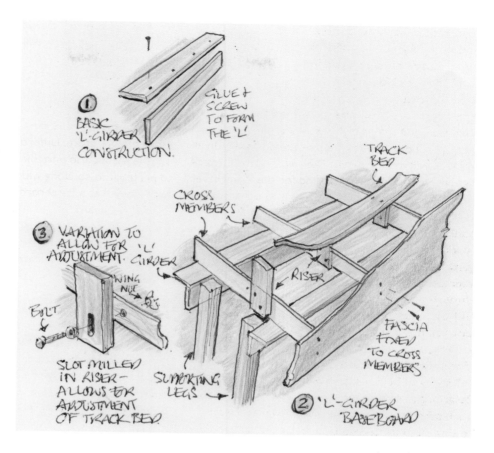

set before any further work was attempted. Although the purchaser can source their own baseboard top material, Model Railway Solutions can supply birch ply baseboard tops as well as supporting legs.

Open-top baseboards are similar in principle, but instead of the framework being completely covered with sheet material, only the area where track is going to be laid (the trackbed) is covered, leaving most of the framing exposed. This saves weight and can allow for scenic features such as cuttings and embankments to be incorporated. Solid- and open-top baseboards form the basis for most portable and exhibition layouts.

A more complex approach is to construct girders or box beams from strips of ply for the longitudinal layout members. Two strips of plywood pinned and glued together as an 'L'-shape will provide strength in both the horizontal and vertical planes, helping to prevent the framework from twisting. Beams are made from two strips of ply spaced apart by soft-

wood blocks, all pinned and glued together, the idea again being to help avoid the frames twisting. Many permanent layouts are built on the 'L'-girder principle, made popular in America in the 1950s by Lyn Westcott, editor of *Model Railroader*. The 'L'-girders can be made from larger-section material such as nominal 1 × 3in (25 × 75mm) timber, glued and toshnailed, or screwed together to provide a very strong and rigid framework. Joists are fixed to the 'L'-girder subframe and risers attached to the joists to carry the trackbed. There are several advantages to this method of baseboard construction:

- It can be economical with regard to the amount of material used, especially for large layouts.
- Carpentry does not have to be precise – there are no butt joints, as in conventional baseboards.
- Joists can be left oversize and cut back later – useful where curved layout edges are required.

Baseboard kits provide a quick and convenient way of assembling the foundation for your layout – adding a ply top will give a typical flat-earth baseboard, while an open baseboard will have just the track base added, leaving the rest of the frames exposed. The legs are recycled from a previous layout.

The proposed 'Harbour Gates' layout mocked up on the two assembled baseboards – these would have been solid top, with scenic treatment finished as a typical harbour or dockside. The group of buildings has been assembled to provide a backdrop with a suitable marine atmosphere.

B&R Model Railways
Tel: 01494 580036
email: info@bandrmodelrailways.co.uk
www.bandrmodelrailways.co.uk

Elite Baseboards
www.elitebaseboards.net

The Goods Yard
Tel: 07930 557601
email: info@thegoodsyard.co.uk
www.thegoodsyard.co.uk

Grainge & Hodder Ltd
Laser-cutting, laser-cut baseboards
Tel: 0121 559 5967
email: sales@graingeandhodder.com
www.graingeandhodder.co.uk

Tim Horn
Laser-cut 'Lite' baseboards and accessories
Tel: 07920 510890
www.timhorn.co.uk

Mike's Joinery Ltd
Tel: 01516 040549
Mobile: 07881 524946

email: mikesjoinery@hotmail.com
www: mikesjoinery-wirral.co.uk

Model Railway Baseboards
Tel: 01223 864029
email: mail@loco-boxes.co.uk
www.model-railway-baseboards.webplus.net

Model Railway Solutions
Tel: 01202 798068
email: info@modelrailwaysolutions.co.uk
www.modelrailwaysolutions.co.uk

Model Scenery Supplies
Tel: 01263 588570
www.modelscenerysupplies.co.uk

PLS (Professional Layout Services)
Tel: 0115 9266290
Mobile: 07988 110722
email: enquiries@pls-layouts.co.uk
www.pls-layouts.co.uk

White Rose Modelworks
Tel: 01677 422444
email: info@whiterosemodelworks.co.uk
www.whiterosemodelworks.co.uk

- Versatility – it is easier to relocate joists and risers where necessary; risers can be arranged to be adjustable to give an exceptional level base for the track.
- Allows for scenery to be easily constructed, especially where there are great variations in ground level.

Finally, for diorama-sized or other small layouts, an alternative material that has become popular in recent years is foamboard. This lightweight material is easily cut with a sharp knife against a straight edge and glued to form surprisingly strong and rigid structures, although it is not recommended for large areas of baseboard.

THE FIRST LAW OF WORKBENCH DYNAMICS

'As work expands to fill available time, so clutter expands to fill available work space.'

You really do not need lavish facilities to build a kit, or scratch-build a model. A larger workbench is not necessarily a good thing and many fine models have been built on the kitchen or dining-room table, or on a modelling tray perched on the knees in front of the television. Following a house move some years ago, I ended up with a generous amount of space and installed a much larger workbench – the result attracted more

The first law of workbench dynamics in action. MICK NICHOLSON

This working area neatly combines bench, shelving for part-finished projects, plus chest of drawers for kits and other bits and pieces.

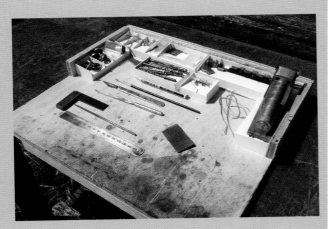

Developing the work tray concept. MICK NICHOLSON

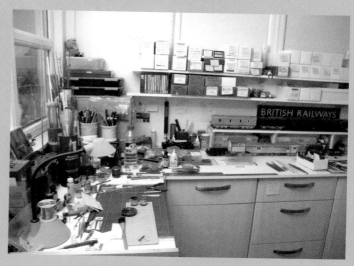

ABOVE: *A large work area can invite clutter.*

LEFT: *Storing work trays in the workshop.* MICK NICHOLSON

The answer – a smaller and neater work bench.

clutter and left little room for modelmaking. Needless to say, it was replaced with a much smaller work area and modelmaking resumed.

The concept of the modelling tray has been further developed by modeller and author Mick Nicholson, who uses a series of homemade trays on which different projects can be worked. Open-top containers hold small components, nuts, bolts, tools, drills and so on. The work trays can be stored in wooden racking in the workshop without the need to clear away tools or workpiece – leaving the actual workbench clear and clutter free!

CHAPTER FOUR

PRACTICAL LAYOUT PLANNING

Having considered how much space is available for a layout, how much time you have available to build it and how much you can afford to spend on it, it is now time to get down to some practical planning. This is probably the most important part of building a layout, as mistakes spotted now can easily be corrected – when the layout is built, mistakes may be difficult or impossible to put right and consequently the layout may have a very short life. Many plans have been published over the years for 'layouts in small spaces', 'minimal space' or 'micro' layouts, although it has to be said that any resemblance to prototype practice usually goes out of the window with most of them. This is due in the main to trying to squeeze a station into what is fundamentally a ridiculously small space. Even the smallest full-size branch-line stations made extravagant use of comparatively cheap land, with plenty of space for run-round loops, sidings, goods

Metro-Vick Co-Bo D5703 runs into the Up Goods Loop at 'Gifford Street'. Although planning is essential before starting to build your layout, things do not always go according to plan. It was originally intended to have a station and loop lines at this end of the layout, but this was altered to include a tunnel based on Summit West on the Leeds to Manchester route. PAUL BASON, COURTESY BRITISH RAILWAY MODELLING

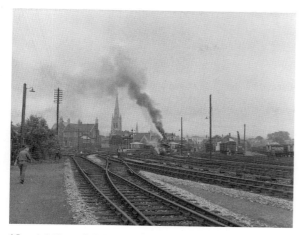

'Castle' Class 4-6-0 No.7029 Clun Castle *prepares to leave a deserted Cheltenham Spa St James station on 12 June 1965, with a Sunday school special to Weston-super-Mare – the last steam-hauled train to leave the station. The photograph gives a good idea of the amount of land required by a medium-sized station and goods yard.* ROY TAYLOR/JOHN EMERSON COLLECTION

shed, loco facilities, cattle dock, coal siding and so on. The problem most modellers are faced with is how to distil a full-size layout into the often far too small space at our disposal.

NO NEED TO THINK BIG

A good first step is to make a list of all the features you wish to include in your idealized layout – for example, goods shed, loco shed, cattle dock, coal sidings, number of platforms and so on. Then, go through the list and break it down into 'must have' features and what it would be nice to include if space is available, in order to whittle down your original list into something that is more feasible. Ask yourself: Do I really need an engine shed? Would a water crane at the end of the platform suffice? Is there room for a goods shed? Can I fit in the number of platforms? What about space for a turntable? Do I really need a station? The last question may seem absurd, but if your interest is mainly shunting freight stock, a 'shunting plank' type of layout might be the ideal solution, as it dispenses with a station and its associated facilities. The setting for this type of layout can vary from an

industrial complex to steel works, or quarries and dockside, but all are characterized by sharp curves with small tank locomotives fussing around. A layout of this type can provide hours of absorbing operation.

Many layouts with an industrial theme have been built in a variety of scales and gauges and can provide plenty of interest for operators and spectators alike. However, an equally good alternative for cramped sites is the urban branch terminus. As land in town and city centres was expensive, the railway companies would only acquire the minimum amount they required, often cramming all the necessary facilities into a narrow, confined area. Many urban sites often had the built-in bonus of being situated in cuttings with high retaining walls and overbridges, which provide ready-made scenic divides and backdrops for the modeller. A small urban terminus would provide an ideal subject for a pre-Grouping layout, where small tank locos and short trains of four- or six-wheel coaches would be the order of the day. For later periods, steam auto-trains or diesel units would be suitable, where you could make full use of DCC sound. And for those really strapped for space, the Heljan AC Cars four-wheel railbus is ideal.

Regardless of size, there are several important and absolute dimensions you need to adhere to if you are to avoid later problems when trying to get the full potential from your layout. First is the space between parallel tracks – the 'six foot' on the full-size railway. If you are using ready-to-lay track and pointwork such as Peco, this will already be set for you. If you are constructing your own track, it should not be less than 45mm (1.8in), although you may wish to increase this value, especially on sharp curves. Next is the length of pointwork – for example, a Peco O-gauge point is 14.5in (368mm) long, so a crossover will be just under 2ft 6in (762mm) overall. These dimensions are critical, for example on a 4ft (1,219mm) long baseboard a point positioned at the edge of the board will only give you an effective siding length of just 19in (483mm). This is because you will need to make an allowance for the fouling point. That is the point beyond which trains or rolling stock on parallel lines

SOME IDEAS FOR INDUSTRIAL LAYOUTS

General industry	Car/vehicle manufacturing plant (for example, BL, Morris, Rover)
	Chocolate factory – Cadbury (Bournville), Fry's (Keynsham), Rowntree (York)
	Metal box company – lots of van traffic
	Nuclear flask loading yard
	Paper mill (for example, Bowaters – Kent)
	Scrapyard – (for example, Cohen's of Kettering)
Heavy industry	Aluminium smelter (for example, Fort William)
	Chemical works (for example, British Cellanese Ltd)
	Coke works (for example, Manvers Main)
	Colliery – NCB (National Coal Board)
	Glass works (for example, Pilkington Brothers)
	Iron/steel works (for example, BSC Corby)
	Oil refinery
	Pipe/tube works (for example, Stanton)
	Tinplate smelter
Miscellaneous	Civil engineer's yard
	Gas works – almost any town
	Harbour/docks
	Military and ordnance depots
	Potato farm – mostly narrow gauge (for example, Smith's in Lincolnshire)
	Sewage farm (for example, Bradford)
Quarries, etc.	Block/paving distributor (for example, Plasmoor)
	Brickworks
	Quarry – stone, iron ore, aggregates and so on
	Sandpit – mostly narrow-gauge lines

will obstruct each other, effectively the length of another point. It will be seen that this dimension becomes increasingly critical when planning run-round loops.

Many small layout plans ignore the run-round loop, but this is one of the most fundamental parts of a layout. How else can you get the locomotive from one end of a train to the other? The only real exceptions are if you are using a suitable dodge to get round this inconvenient fact (such as an 'off-stage' cassette or fiddle yard), or if you are modelling current practice with diesel or electric units. There is no set dimension for the length of a run-round loop – either it is made long enough to hold the longest train you are likely to run, or the longest train you will be able to run on your layout will be whatever you can fit into the loop – so you will need to know the dimensions of locomotives and rolling stock likely to be used on the layout:

0-6-0T (8in/203mm); 2-6-2T (10in/254mm)
4-4-0/Bo-Bo diesel (14in/356mm);
0-6-0 16in/406mm)
Six-wheel coach (12in/305mm)
57ft coach (16in/406mm)
64ft coach (18in/457mm)
Two-car DMU (36in/915mm)
Four-wheel van/wagon (5 1/2in/140mm)
Large van/wagon (9in/230mm)
'Bogie Bolster' (10in/255mm)

'Central Works', the latest layout to emerge from the 'Loggies'. Following on from their 'Great Train Robbery' diorama, the new layout is based around the exchange sidings at a car manufacturing plant – the Ford plant's diesel shunter was scratch-built by Simon Bolton. DAVID COASBY

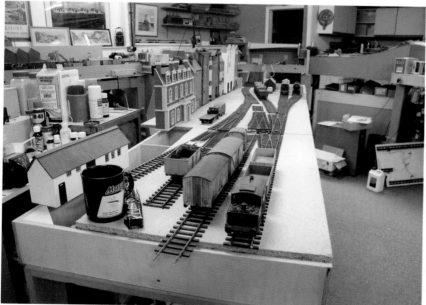

An important part of layout planning is blocking in track, pointwork and buildings to gauge clearances, length of sidings, run-round loop and so on – something to eat and drink is also a vital part of the planning process!

Whilst layouts can easily be planned using software such as Templot, XTrkCad or 3rd PlanIt, I still prefer to draw out the layout plan and then transfer the full-size design to a roll of lining paper. Whichever way is chosen, it is still advisable before committing the final design to the baseboard to 'block out' the design on the floor with lengths of track and points (or track and point templates, or computer printout), a loco and some rolling stock, and cardboard mock-up buildings and structures. This will enable you to notice any tight spots, clearance issues and other potential operational problems before construction commences. It is also a good idea to mark the position of baseboard cross members to see if they will interfere with any under-baseboard point or signal motors or rodding and wiring runs – these can then be repositioned if required.

Personally, unless modelling a prototype location, I do not like slavishly following 'absolute' layout plans that are planned to the minutest detail, preferring a more fluid approach that allows alterations as you go along. It is also good practice to spend time 'looking' – in other words, step back and look at the blocked-in plan from all angles. Using a phone or digital camera as a digital notebook as you go along is also recommended, especially when track is being laid. Looking at the resulting photographs on a computer screen at high magnification may uncover horrors you might not spot with the unaided eye. If it doesn't look right, alter it, and if it still doesn't look right, do not be afraid to bin it and start again!

THE SPACE-SAVING COMPACT LAYOUT

Whilst the very minimum size of layout you can get away with will not be much bigger than a diorama, operational potential will be extremely limited. And without a run-round loop, shunting will consist of merely shuffling a few wagons around. Operating potential will increase if a little more space is available, for example 8–10ft (2.4–3m) will enable a reasonable shunting-type layout or a very small station to be produced. The various schemes outlined below are taken from ideas for layout projects that have been sketched out over the years and which I hope will prove useful jumping-off points for your own projects.

'HARBOUR GATES'
(8 × 2ft/2.4 × 0.6m)

This proposed scheme actually got as far as being mocked up on a pair of baseboards. The basic idea assumes an available space of around 10–12ft (3–3.7m) where the layout can be sited, along the length of one side of a bedroom, for example. When planning this layout it seemed that there were two distinct ways in which to approach it. First, a line running in from the right-hand side with a fan of three or four sidings would be fine for shuffling wagons around, but with no run-round loop operation would be limited and possibly would soon become boring. The second idea was to again bring the line in from the right-hand side, but this time as double track and part of a run-round loop (the rest of the loop being 'off-stage', with the

Colin French built 'Ledsam Street Yard', which is more of an operational diorama than a minimum-space shunting-plank layout. PAUL BASON, COURTESY RAILWAY MODELLER

The 'Harbour Gates' shunting layout mocked up on two 4 × 2ft (1.2 × 0.6m) baseboards to see if the concept works – a small loco depot was added to provide basic facilities for a collection of small shunting locos, but could equally be used for industrial sidings, timber yard, oil depot and so on. The two tracks would have led to a small cassette fiddle yard.

addition of a small add-on board to take a sector plate or cassette storage system). With the addition of a lengthy kickback road leading to a small loco depot, this seemed to offer the best solution to the problem.

The two baseboards are each 4 × 2ft (1.2 × 0.6m) and built from easily assembled kits with a solid top added. For exhibition use, the baseboard edge could be finished as the dockside. The layout is supported on redundant legs recycled from 'Gifford Street'. A layout of this size should not take too long to build, although the number of points required would initially make it a fairly expensive exercise. However, it is well worthwhile trawling eBay, or the bring and buy stalls at model railway shows in search of a bargain or two, although in the case of second-hand points care

needs to be taken in selecting the best examples. For this project, a job lot of second-hand points and track was acquired at around a third of the cost of buying new, although a fair amount of time was subsequently spent on cleaning up the rails, removing solder joints and the odd track pin before being deemed suitable for reuse. It was decided that for a small layout of this size the track would be laid directly on to the ply baseboard surface instead of using any underlay.

Small tank locomotives would be ideal for a dockside scheme such as this, plus the use of DCC sound and suitable seaside sound effects would add to the overall atmosphere. Rolling stock would be confined to suitable vans, open wagons, containers, tank wagons and of course plenty of fish vans.

Larger than the 'Harbour Gates' scheme, 'Penpoll Quay' depicts the quayside terminus of a Cornish china clay branch, always an interesting subject for an O-gauge layout, providing plenty of opportunity for shunting. The storage roads are accessed through a bridge at the rear of the layout and hidden behind the retaining walls.

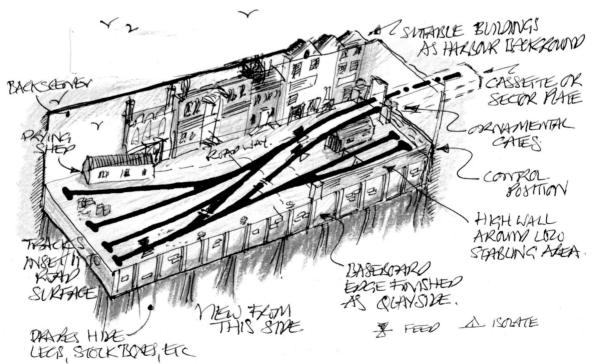

The basic idea for 'Harbour Gates' sketched out – the plan was then blocked in on a pair of baseboards to see if everything would fit into an area of around 8 × 2ft (2.4 × 0.6m) and any adjustments made.

Item	Qty		
Peco L/H points	2	Baseboard legs	3
Peco R/H points	4	Peco track pins	I pack
Peco Streamline track	6yd	Peco rail joiners	I pack
Point motors	6	Peco insulated rail joiners	I pack
On/off slider switches	6 (if not using point motors)	Baseboard dowels	I pair
		Coach bolt/washer/wing nut	2 × 8mm
On/off toggle switches	4		
4 × 2ft baseboard	2 kits plus tops (birch ply)	Wire (various colours) for electrics, plugs and sockets, solder tag strips, solder, screws, white glue (PVA). Controller/transformer	

Hunslet 0-4-0 diesel mechanical shunter No.11502 – an ideal model of a type specifically designed to work over the tight curves of dockside tramways on the Eastern Region of BR.

'ISLEBROOK QUARRIES'
(8 × 8ft/2,438 × 2,438mm)

Track-plan illustrator Ian Wilson came up with the basic premise for this 7mm-scale project layout with an industrial theme for *British Railway Modelling* some years ago, taking as inspiration the ironstone railways of his native Northamptonshire. For an O-gauge scheme it would provide plenty of interest in a modest amount of space, being constructed on four baseboards in an area measuring 8 × 8ft (2.4 × 2.4m) approximately, with the operator sitting snugly inside the layout. The original plan envisaged hand-built track to represent a lightly laid industrial line using flat-bottom rail, although it could be re-planned to take advantage of the new Peco O-gauge Setrack system that has since appeared. It would also

lend itself to being built as a narrow-gauge feeder line connecting with the standard-gauge main line, although this would necessitate modelling some sort of loading bank for transhipping the iron ore from the narrow-gauge system to standard-gauge wagons in the exchange sidings.

The line is assumed to be on a rising gradient from the quarry face to the exchange sidings, with the connection to the BR main line conveniently 'off-stage'. As drawn, there is only enough room for a longish head-shunt concealed behind the quarry face for shunting the exchange sidings, although this could be replaced by a cassette system. All operations would be on the 'one engine in steam' principle, although adding a loop in the main line would provide for more flexible operation. Rolling stock would comprise wooden or

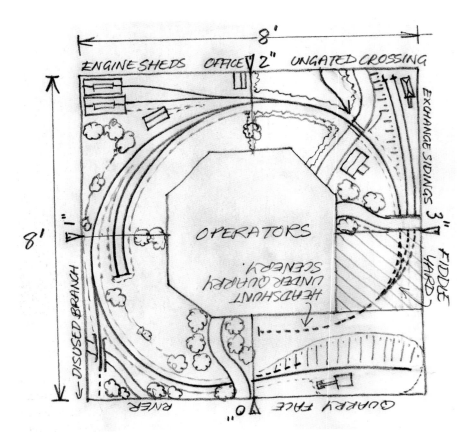

Ian Wilson's original sketch plan for the 'Islebrook Quarries' layout.

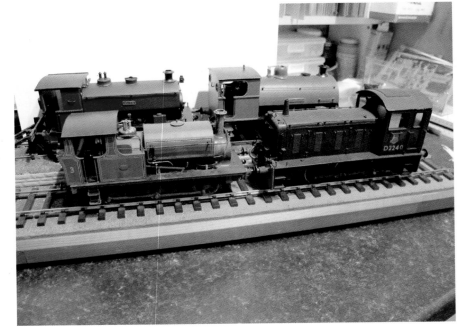

A collection of locos suitable for an O-gauge industrial layout: Andrew Barclay 14in cylinder 0-4-0ST Ruth built from a Tower Models starter kit; Peckett 0-4-0ST Fearless built from a Springside Models kit; Drewry 0-6-0 diesel mechanical shunter No.D2240 built from a Vulcan Models kit; and Ixion ready-to-run Hudswell Clarke 0-6-0ST.

The real thing – Peckett 'E' Class 0-4-0ST No.7 Beaufort receiving attention at Pontardulais tinplate works in the late 1950s.
ROY TAYLOR/JOHN EMERSON COLLECTION

steel iron ore and mineral wagons, the odd van for stores and open wagons for loco coal and ash disposal, plus a brake van or two for trains marshalled in the exchange sidings. For added interest, a couple of old four-wheel coaches could provide a workman's train to and from the quarry face.

The locomotive fleet would consist of small but powerful 0-4-0 or 0-6-0 tanks, the Minerva Peckett or Kerr-Stuart being an ideal candidate, and DCC sound could be employed to full advantage. The exchange sidings might see the appearance of the odd BR steam or diesel loco, while for a more modern approach small diesel shunters could replace the industrial 'kettles'. As there are plenty of industrial-type locos available as kits, a varied stud could be built up over a period of time and the loco shed provides an ideal setting to display all those lovely RTR tank locomotives, or to show off the latest work of art fresh off the workbench.

If some room was available it would be possible to add the BR tracks next to the exchange sidings, although unless the amount of space was considerable, these would obviously only be for static display. There is plenty of scope for scenic development and with the addition of a face shovel the quarry face in particular would make an impressive scenic feature.

For various reasons, the concept was not taken up and it remains unbuilt, although Ian keeps threatening actually to get round to building it! However, an industrial scheme of this nature would make an unusual and absorbing project for an individual or group to build.

SOME LARGER LAYOUT SCHEMES

'HAYLEY MILLS MKVI' (16 × 2ft/4,877 × 610mm)

With the increasing availability of DCC sound for O-gauge locos, it became fashionable to build exhibition layouts based on locomotive depots. Some serious thought was given to joining the fray by building a relatively small stabling point, the inspiration coming from my original 4mm-scale 'Hayley Mills' layout. This represented a refuelling point for diesel locomotives and was built in about six weeks on a well-seasoned plank found in my parents' garden! However, the 7mm version would have used a much more conventional approach with plywood baseboard kits. It was assumed that the stabling point was built on the remains of the old steam shed and, not content with a 'flat-earth' approach, variations in ground level would be introduced, whilst additional scenic interest would be created by modelling the track as if it had been truncated at some time, with the remains of bridge wing walls over either a road or canal – I had not actually made my mind up by the time this scheme was abandoned.

Another feature would have been a CCE siding complete with ballast tip and a dumped loco or two, something almost never seen in 7mm, but making use of a couple of partially built loco kits that were on the workbench at the time, suitably dressed up to look as if they were en route to the scrap yard. Needless to say, this never happened, although the ballast-tip idea will eventually make it on to 'Gifford Street' as part of the scenic treatment for the New

Yard. It was envisaged that C&L plain track would be used, preferably with hand-built pointwork, although employing Peco points would save time. The double slip on the headshunt/run-round road, whilst being slightly more complex to build and wire up, is a valuable space-saving device. As with the previous two plans, operation would have been all DCC. Unfortunately, this scheme eventually foundered when an almost identical 4mm layout plan was published in one of the model railway magazines – is nothing sacred?

'A TOUCH OF WHIMSEY' (26ft × 2ft 6in/7.9 × 0.75m)

This one may well make it to completion as a possible long-term replacement for 'Gifford Street' if the need to downsize rises. The Forest of Dean provides a rich source of inspiration for railway modellers, with a tangle of Midland, GWR and independent colliery

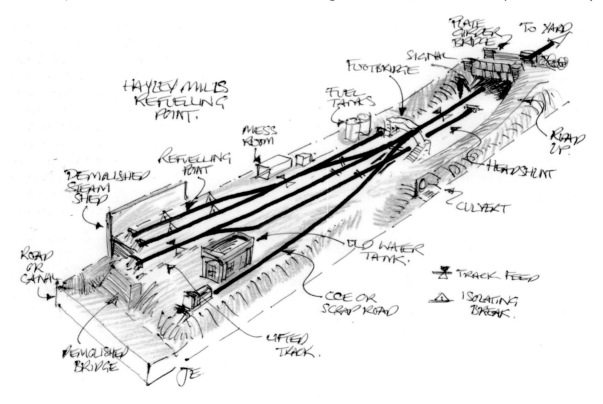

Sketch plan of the concept for the 'Hayley Mills' stabling/refuelling point, developed from the original 4mm-scale layout. Just the place to display some of those nice DCC sound-fitted diesels.

A small diesel depot can provide the perfect setting for a collection of diesel locomotives. This is 'Lochty Lane' stabling point from Ian Futers, who has made a speciality of building small O-gauge layouts.

lines. The introduction of Lionheart's 16 ton minerals and 14 ton ex-Air Ministry tank wagons provided the impetus to look at a suitable scheme based in the Whimsey area, where Berry Wiggens had a bitumen depot in the old station. The scheme does not purport to be an accurate model of the location but hopefully to give a flavour of the area, with a truncated branch line and junction leading to a colliery. The station is still in use with an infrequent service, there is a small yard for local goods traffic, a bay platform for parcels and the like, and mineral trains on the colliery line – empties in, loaded out, wagons

being swapped over in the fiddle yard, which serves both the main line and the colliery branch.

Motive power would be a mixture of GWR pannier types as well as 'Small Prairie' and 'Mogul', plus Midland 0-6-0s. Rolling stock would be mainly steel or wooden-bodied 16 ton minerals, plus a selection of varied freight stock and of course bitumen tank wagons for Berry Wiggens. As some of these would need to be scratch-built or kit-bashed, this would definitely be a suitable scheme for the dedicated freight man. Passengers would be catered for by a two-coach set drawn from a mixture of Hawksworth,

'HAYLEY MILLS MkVI' SHOPPING LIST

Item	Qty
Peco L/H points	1
Peco R/H points	5
Peco double slip	1
Peco Streamline track	12yd
Point motors	8
On/off toggle switches	4
4 × 2ft baseboard	2 kits plus tops
Baseboard legs	3

Peco track pins	1 pack
Peco rail joiners	1 pack
Peco insulated rail joiners	2 packs
Baseboard dowels	1 pair
Coach bolt/washer/wing nut	2 × 8mm

Wire (various colours) for electrics, plugs and sockets, solder tag strips, solder, screws, white glue (PVA).
Controller/transformer

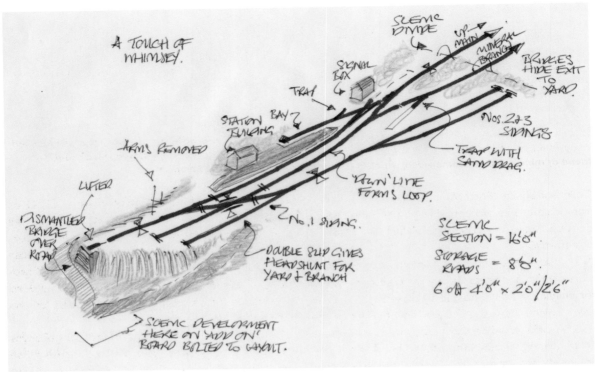

Sketch plan of an idea for a layout based in the Forest of Dean – dubbed 'A Touch of Whimsey', as it is fictional and not based on any particular location.

The small station at Coleford in the Forest of Dean would make an ideal subject for a small- to medium-sized layout.
ROY TAYLOR/JOHN EMERSON
COLLECTION

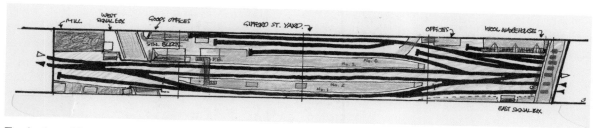

Track plan of 'Utterly', the first O-gauge layout with which I was involved – although the project never reached completion, it still looks a hugely workable plan. Regrettably, there are no decent photographs, although a friend of mine did shoot some video, which is the only record I have of the layout.

Collett or Stanier 'Porthole' corridor stock cascaded from main-line service, providing a welcome change from the obligatory GWR branch-line fare of 'B set' or auto-train.

This scheme would need a lot of detailed scenic treatment to bring it to life and the timescale needed for building it would most likely make it a long-term solo project. However, if taken on by a group, the various tasks could be delegated, with one team for track building, another for wiring and electrics, and yet another for scenics and so on. In this way, and by running the groups in parallel, the project could be completed in a much reduced timescale.

'UTTERLY'

This first excursion into O gauge turned out not to be the layout it was supposed to be! My first thoughts had centred on a small shunting yard, but after seeing several interesting small 7mm layouts at exhibitions, it evolved into a branch-line terminus and goods yard. Then the local club decided to build a large O-gauge test track, so the design was altered again to become a through station. This could either be dropped into the club's test track to give a 35 × 15ft (10.6 × 4.6m) main-line scheme, or, by using a fiddle yard at each end for through running, be exhibited as a standalone layout.

In the event, the test track was never completed, so 'Utterly' remained an end-to-end layout. Constructed as a group project on four 5 × 3ft (1,524 × 914mm) ply baseboards, using Peco 'Streamline' plain track and hand-built points, it proved remarkably effective as a setting for main-line running, although trains were necessarily limited in length to the longest cassettes available in the two fiddle yards.

Although built before the introduction of DCC, up to four trains could be operated at once, a limited amount of cab-control being available from the controllers installed for running the Up and Down main lines, the relief line and shunting the goods yard, providing plenty of action for spectators at exhibitions. The station facilities included a bay platform for parcels traffic.

'Utterly' remained in an unfinished state after my relocation to Lincolnshire to start work with *British Railway Modelling*. After a period in storage, the layout was eventually broken up, although parts of the goods yard and all of the buildings were incorporated into the present 'Gifford Street'. Was it an expensive folly? On balance, I would say that no layout is ever really a waste of time and money, as along the way invaluable lessons will be learned and experience gained. More than likely at least some of the track and points can be recovered, any locos and rolling stock acquired can be deployed on the next project, as can buildings, figures and other details. Railway modellers are the ultimate recyclers! However, 'Utterly' would make an ideal project for a group of friends to work on, although the thoroughly workable design would really come into its own if developed into a continuous circuit as a large club project.

FLIGHTS OF FANCY

Although the above schemes are all freelance in nature, some modellers prefer to build a layout based on a suitable prototype location. There are several advantages to this approach: for instance, signalling can be based directly on the siting of the prototype;

it may be possible to measure and photograph buildings and other structures where they are still extant; photographs or film footage taken at various periods are usually available; and the frequency and type of train services can easily be determined from *Working Time Tables* and other documents. However, there can also be problems modelling an actual location, the most common being trying to compress the sheer size of a prototype layout into manageable proportions. For example, at Malvern Road in Cheltenham the East and West signal boxes are within easy walking distance of each other, being only 540yd (500m) apart. However, as this would scale out at 36ft (10m) in 7mm scale, unless there is unlimited space available, the art of compromise will often have to be brought into play, with distances being reduced. Sometimes selective compression may also have to be used in the track layout itself, resulting in a reduction of the number of sidings or other tracks and so on. Care must be taken with the use of selective compression when modelling actual locations, or the resulting model may no longer resemble the prototype location, but merely become a reflection of it. However, this can also be turned to the modeller's advantage by reducing or compressing a prototype track layout or location and using it as the basis for a freelance project. Prototype layouts can provide some satisfying models, so to end with here are a couple of examples taken from my interest in railways in the Cheltenham area.

LECKHAMPTON

Leckhampton on the outskirts of Cheltenham was on the GWR's Cheltenham & Banbury direct line to Kingham, at one time the shortest route to London for those not wanting to use the prestigious 'Cheltenham Flyer'. In pre-Grouping days it also saw the 'Ports to Ports Express' from Newcastle to Cardiff, the station providing a Cheltenham stop for passengers, although the GWR saw fit to ignore the fact that it was located several miles from the town centre, misleading unwary passengers by naming it Cheltenham South. As a consequence, the platforms at Leckhampton are comparatively long for a small station, so on a model it would not look out of place in a main-

line scheme. Traffic on the line was particularly heavy in both world wars and these periods could form the basis of an interesting layout with a wide variety of locomotives and stock.

Trains from Andover and Southampton also called at Leckhampton, having traversed the Midland & South Western Junction Railway route (the 'Tiddley Dyke'), joining the GWR at Andoversford. In later years, this brought U Class 'Moguls' from the Southern Region into Cheltenham. Basic goods facilities were provided, a small yard serving coal and scrap merchants. Drawings of the goods shed, signal box and road bridge were published by Eric Illett many years ago and at one time were available from Peco. The road bridge situated at the 'town' end provides a useful scenic break, although the bridge carrying Old Bath Road over the line at the other end of the station is a good quarter of a mile or so away. Known locally as 'Pilley Bridge', it achieved national fame in 1954 when it became the last wartime-damaged bridge to be repaired in the UK. However, with a little selective compression this could also be used as an effective scenic break. Leckhampton also appeared in the BTF film *Mishap*. Renamed 'Aysbury', there are useful shots of trains on the line, as well as interior views of the signal box and station building.

THE 'TIDDLEY DYKE' BAY

Where space is at a premium an alternative solution might be the 'bits of layout' concept where only a part of a prototype location is modelled. This could be particularly useful for someone whose interests are primarily building rolling stock or locomotives, providing a working diorama where the latest models could be displayed, for example. The old Ladies College and M&SWJR bay platforms at Lansdown station on the former Midland Railway route could provide an interesting subject for a small project. Situated at the side of the main station, in pre-Grouping days the main bay platform was used by M&SWJR departures (the 'Tiddley Dyke' bay), the furthest bay road being known as the horse box or Ladies College bay, where luggage for the college

'Jubilee' Class 4-6-0 No.45660 Rooke heads the northbound 'Devonian' into Cheltenham's Lansdown station on the Bristol–Birmingham main line. Many of the locations in Cheltenham are good for modelling – the bay platforms to the left are where the 'Tiddley Dyke' (MSWJR) trains left for Southampton.
ROY TAYLOR/JOHN EMERSON COLLECTION

was loaded and unloaded at the beginning and end of each term.

In LMS days, these bay platform roads became the refuge of elderly Midland Railway 2-4-0s working out their last days, at least one locomotive becoming a local celebrity. Post-war, the bays gradually saw less use until they were finally taken out of use and the main platform lengthened to accommodate the newly introduced HST sets. However, plans have been outlined to build new 270m-long bay platforms on the site to take the new IEP (Intercity Express Programme) units, which would bring the history of the bay platforms full circle.

BUILDING A LAYOUT 'OFF THE SHELF'

Finally, if after reading through this you think it is still too difficult, it is increasingly possible these days to buy almost everything you need for an O-gauge layout off the shelf, ranging from baseboards (either kits or ready-made), to all of the stock, locomotives, buildings, scenics and so on – although you will still have to lay the track and wire it up. But even if you are totally ham-fisted, there are many businesses only too happy to build your baseboards, or construct a complete layout for you.

Up the Junction – Filling an Awkward Corner

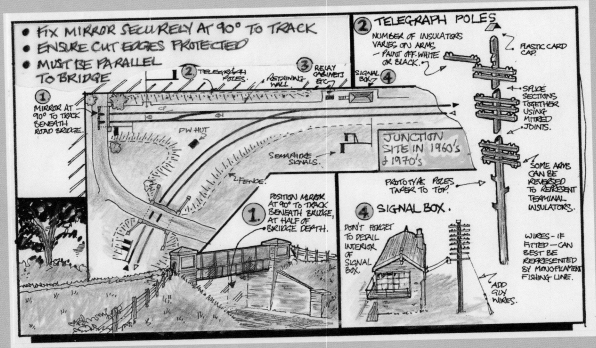

- FIX MIRROR SECURELY AT 90° TO TRACK
- ENSURE CUT EDGES PROTECTED
- MUST BE PARALLEL TO BRIDGE

① MIRROR AT 90° TO TRACK BENEATH ROAD BRIDGE.

② TELEGRAPH POLES

③ RELAY CABINETS ETC

RETAINING WALL

SIGNAL BOX ④

CP

PW HUT

SEMAPHORE SIGNALS.

FENCE.

JUNCTION SITE IN 1960's & 1970's

POSITION MIRROR AT 90° TO TRACK BENEATH BRIDGE, AT HALF OF BRIDGE DEPTH.

② TELEGRAPH POLES

NUMBER OF INSULATORS VARIES ON ARMS – PAINT OFF-WHITE OR BLACK.

PLASTIC CARD CAP.

SPLICE SECTIONS TOGETHER USING MITRED JOINTS.

SOME ARMS CAN BE REVERSED TO REPRESENT TERMINAL INSULATORS.

PROTOTYPE POLES TAPER TO TOP

④ SIGNAL BOX.

DON'T FORGET TO DETAIL INTERIOR OF SIGNAL BOX.

WIRES – IF FITTED – CAN BEST BE REPRESENTED BY MONOFILAMENT FISHING LINE.

ADD GUY WIRES.

Not sure what to do with an awkward corner site? How about a dummy junction – adds an air of importance and a mirror under the bridge will make the tracks appear to go straight through the wall. To complete the illusion, make sure that the mirror is at 90 degrees to the tracks and halfway under the bridge and parallel to it.

Ten Tips for Better Layouts

1. Ensure that run-round loops are long enough to hold the longest train you are likely to run.

2. At a branch terminus, the run-round loop will more than likely run into a short siding or headshunt. At a minimum, this will need to be long enough to hold the largest locomotive likely to run on the line.

3. Try to avoid kickback sidings wherever possible. A kickback siding will be impossible to shunt if stock is standing on the line it leads from.

4. Prototype railways avoid facing points and crossovers wherever possible – so should you! However, sometimes you can't, for example at junctions and loops.

5. Using double slips and curved or 'Y' points can save valuable space on small layouts.

6. Regularly 'block in' track, pointwork and buildings to gauge clearances, length of sidings and so on.

7. Record progress and check details with a 'digital' notebook.

8. Ensure that all wiring is complete and thoroughly checked before ballasting the track.

9. Even with DCC, keep track and wheels clean and use a light touch on the controller.

10. If it does not look right or work properly, it may be easier to scrap the layout and start again.

CHAPTER FIVE

SUCCESSFUL SCENICS

MODEL WHAT YOU SEE ...

An important dictum is to model what you see, not what you think you see. Railway engineers soon realized that railways worked best if they could be kept almost level, without any severe gradients, so they avoided hills or crossing deep valleys wherever possible. If there was no way round, then they had to dig a cutting or bore a tunnel, the spoil often being used to fill in low-lying ground to avoid expensive bridges and viaducts. So whilst railways are comparatively level, they run through areas of continually undulating ground, sometimes higher than the railway, sometimes lower.

Unless you have a vast amount of space at your disposal, any scenic development on the average O-gauge layout will more than likely be limited to whatever is immediately beyond the boundary fence or retaining wall and probably will be more urban than rural – if you really feel the need to model the railway fully in the landscape, then N gauge might be the better choice!

Most layouts will probably have been built on a flat solid-top baseboard surface without much regard for future scenic development, so any scenic features added afterwards are in danger of looking something of an afterthought. As naturally flat areas of any great

The railway in the landscape – the GWR station at Crumlin Low Level seen from a train crossing Crumlin viaduct has all the elements of a model railway. Sadly, much of this scene has long since passed into history, including the station and the viaduct itself, leaving little trace of a once extensive railway network.
ROY TAYLOR/JOHN EMERSON COLLECTION

A Heljan Brush Type 4 emerges from Summit West Tunnel on 'Gifford Street'. Building a realistic tunnel makes an interesting modelling project, is certainly not at all difficult and at the same time helps disguise our 'flat earth' baseboards. Details such as speed restriction sign, milepost and cable trunking help to complete the scene.

As the baseboards for 'Gifford Street' are all solid top, the ground level on the approach to the tunnel had to be built up, a fairly quick and easy exercise with profiles roughly cut from plywood for the ground contours, retaining wall and tunnel mouth. Thick card, insulation board, foam board or MDF would make suitable alternatives. Profiles are fixed to the baseboard using blocks of wood, glued and screwed, or lengths of scrap aluminium angle, as seen here.

The basic groundwork was blocked in using offcuts of expanded polystyrene packaging cut with an old bread knife and fixed in position with PVA woodworking glue and foam nails. High-density insulation blats are a less messy, but more expensive option (the packaging was free!). Alternatively, you could use a lattice of thin card strips (from cereal packets and the like) hot-glued to the formers, or chicken wire stapled to the profiles and moulded to shape to create the base for the scenery – but wear protective gloves if using this method.

When the polystyrene blocks are thoroughly stuck down, carve to shape with the bread knife – if you have borrowed one from the kitchen, you may have to explain any polystyrene beads and glue residue to the other half! Carving does not have to be exact at this stage and final profiling was completed using a small surform tool, but make sure you have a black bin bag handy to put waste in and vacuum up all debris as you go along.

A hard shell needs to be added to the polystyrene base – I used Woodland Scenics Lightweight Hydrocal, a fast-setting plaster specifically designed for scenic work, but there are plenty of suitable materials available from other manufacturers. The trackbed was protected from spills with old newspapers. Mix the plaster according to the instructions – it is fast-setting, so only mix enough to do an area with which you are comfortable and be prepared to do the rest in several hits. Keep a container of clean water handy to clean the knife and spatula and also to wet any tools used in spreading the plaster. If using the card lattice or wire-netting method, when happy with the shape of the contours, cover with strips of wet plaster bandage.

Every so often it pays to block in scenery, buildings and rolling stock, in order to get an idea of how things should look – even at an advanced stage of construction. A loco and a few mineral wagons have been posed to get a feel for how things should look when finished. If you are not completely satisfied, do not be afraid to alter, rip out, or bin things and redo them at this stage – for example, the culvert and water course on the hillside lead to an aqueduct over the tracks, but at a late stage were removed as they looked contrived. The aqueduct remains!

An overall view of work in progress – the road next to the site of the laundry building on the right was another idea that did not make it on to the finished layout. The main-line tracks are flat bottom, including a hand-built point and Down line relaid on concrete sleepers – all from the Peco 'Streamline' and 'Individulay' ranges.

When dry, the plaster shell was painted with Woodland Scenics paint, again specifically designed for the job, although poster or emulsion paints are good alternatives. The paint does not have to cover thickly, just a thin wash will do, but it will help to show up any imperfections in the plaster shell that need remedial attention.

size are remarkably rare in Britain, we have to disguise our 'flat earth' and inevitably this will be in one direction – up. Building a cutting leading into a bridge or tunnel disguising the exit to the fiddle yard is a good example.

USING OFF THE SHELF SCENICS

Scenic modelling has come a long way from the days of using cement and dyed sawdust and boiling fish glue. Various materials are available today to represent grass embankments or cutting sides, ranging from the old favourite of dyed lint and carpet underlay, to modern ready-to-use commercial grass mats, hanging basket liner and the current favourites, teddy bear fur fabric and static grass. None is necessarily better than any other and all will produce different effects, useful for representing different areas of grass and other foliage. Although there is not a lot of scenic work on 'Gifford Street', the two main materials that have been used are grass and foliage mats (which may prove expensive for large areas) and teddy bear fur fabric.

The 'grass' is teddy bear fur fabric stuck down with PVA glue, then trimmed and painted with a very dilute mix of Precision Doncaster Green. The layout appeared at several shows with the fabric in an unpainted state, which led to occasional bouts of 'layout stroking' by various ladies from the audience!

With the teddy bear fur fabric now trimmed and painted, it is time for the final scenic dressing. PVA glue is first applied over the 'grass' and scenic scatter material applied. Repeat the process until satisfied with the results.

Static grass being applied – the crocodile clip attached to the track completes the path for the static electricity to drive the grass fibres.

There are two ways to apply the fabric – either stick it down, trim and paint (as I did), or trim then paint before sticking down (as Pete Waterman demonstrated on his 'Leamington Spa' layout). In retrospect, the 'Leamington' way probably gives more control over the process, but the 'Gifford Street' method seems to give a random appearance to the finished grass. Whichever, be sure not to give the material an all-over 'short back and sides'. I later found out from Pete that he had come up with a way of representing windblown grass by lightly running a gas torch over the fire-resistant fabric before it was painted and stuck on to the layout – needless to say, I found this out after I had stuck all mine down on very flammable polystyrene blocks.

TREES

Modellers invariably underestimate the size of trees on their layouts and in 7mm scale the largest can be very big indeed. For example, a typical elm can be between 100 and 130ft high at maturity – that would scale out at the best part of 3ft! Then there is the

ABOVE LEFT: The tunnel mouth, retaining walls and wing walls were added using Slater's embossed stone sheets stuck with liberal amounts of PVA glue – any gaps were filled in later with fast-setting glue or filler. I always prime plastic stonework (as well as baseboard surfaces and other scenic areas) with grey emulsion before starting any final painting or weathering, as it provides a good 'ground' for enamels and acrylics. It will also give the finished paintwork better colour rendition – let grey emulsion be your friend!

ABOVE RIGHT: View from inside the finished tunnel. The roof of the tunnel is brick-embossed styrene sheet glued to pre-cut formers, while the walls are Slater's embossed stonework, again fixed with liberal amounts of PVA glue. The stonework around the tunnel mouth was drawn out on a sheet of Plastikard, then cut out and stuck on individually. When complete, the retaining walls and tunnel mouth were primed, before final painting and weathering.

The completed approach to the tunnel, loosely based on Summit Tunnel West on the ex-L&Y Manchester–Leeds route. At exhibitions a 'black box' extension was added behind the tunnel to help block out daylight.

size of the trunk and the spread of the canopy to consider. Model trees of this size would completely dominate any layout, however big, so once again we have to employ the art of compromise. Although several concerns now produce ready-to-use trees for 7mm modellers, it is worth looking at what's also available in 4mm scale – large 4mm-scale trees can make useful small- to medium-sized trees for the 7mm modeller. Where a lot of trees are required, those towards the back of the scene need not be full trees, as only the upper part of the canopy will be visible from normal viewing distance. If using smaller

The other end of the tunnel at an early stage of scenic development – the tracks here lead on to Black Bull Crossing with the pub visible at lower left. The area behind the pub will be covered in large trees – these are really rather small being designed for 4mm-scale layouts, but have been placed to give an idea of what the finished area should look like.

4mm-scale trees, raise up on blocks to make the rear trees appear larger. Finally, do not assume that tree trunks are brown; most will be a grey-green shade with the effects of weather, lichen growth and the like.

Here are the average sizes of some mature trees, with the equivalent 7mm-scale dimensions:

Size	Species	Av.	7mm
Small (up to 25ft)	box, hazel	16ft	4.25in
Medium (25–70ft)	crab apple, hawthorn	30ft	8.25in
	rowan, yew	50ft	13.75in
	whitebeam	65ft	18in
Large (80ft and over)	alder, beech, holly, hornbeam, silver birch, willow	82ft	22.75in
	ash, lime, Scots pine, sessile oak	98ft	27in
	English oak	115ft	31.5in
	elm	130ft	35.75in

EMBANKMENTS

Having looked at how to create effective scenery above track level, how do we go about achieving the same effect below track level? One way is to use the baseboard frame as the lowest point of ground level instead of track level so that the tracks can sit above or below the surrounding ground. On a permanent layout this can easily be achieved with 'L'-girder construction. However, if the layout is portable it can still be done using open frame baseboards, or with a 'dropped' baseboard – particularly useful if you want to model a bridge crossing a river valley for instance.

The profile of the ground contours are built up in exactly the same way as before, using expanded polystyrene or high-density foam used for home insulation – usually pink or blue in colour – which can be sawn and sanded with far less resultant mess. As this can be expensive, a good idea is to look out for a local housing development and see if there are any offcuts being skipped. However, please ask for permission before taking anything out of a skip. The finished contoured ground is then given a thin skim of plaster to provide a smooth surface before further scenic work can take place – I use Woodland Scenics

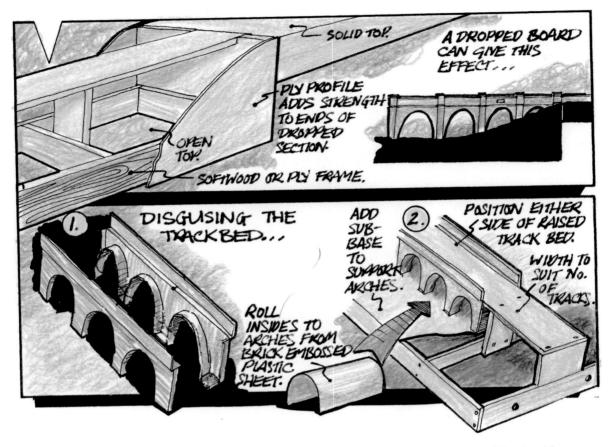

The real world is full of ups and downs but it is quite easy to give your layout different track levels with a dropped section or baseboard to allow the tracks to cross a river or canal, for example. Bridgework can be scratch-built, or there are many commercial parts that can be used.

Lightweight Hydrocal, a fast-setting plaster specifically designed for scenic work, but there are plenty of suitable materials available from other manufacturers.

FENCING

Cuttings and embankments will require some form of boundary fencing. Britain is the only country with a statutory requirement to fence off the railway line, not only to keep livestock from straying on to the railway, but also to prevent railway employees trespassing on to neighbouring land. From the earliest days, a wooden post and rail or post and wire fence was sufficient, usually around 3ft 6in high, with either two wooden rails or five strands of wire. After 1977, the statutory requirement changed so that fences should

be physically capable of preventing trespass, leading to the security-style palisade fencing in use today. One thing to remember with any fence is that the posts remain vertical, even if the fence is built on rising ground – the rails or wire will slope according to ground condition. It should also be remembered that the railway boundary fence will almost invariably be at the *top* of a cutting, but at the *bottom* of an embankment.

Some railway companies developed their own distinctive style of fencing, notably the Midland with its diagonal paling design, or the widespread use of concrete on the Southern. Fortunately, various styles of fencing are available commercially for O-gauge modellers. For those modelling the Southern Railway or BR Southern Region, typical SR concrete panel

Using the principle of the dropped baseboard on 'Gifford Street'. Part of the main framework has been removed to create a short embankment and bridge under the railway. Blocks of expanded polystyrene were glued in place and shaped to form the land dropping below track level. Not ideal, but a lot of this free material was to hand!

Getting rid of the traditional baseboard facia is another way of disguising a 'flat earth' baseboard. The ground level drops away on this side of the yard where the coal drops are situated and will continue at this level around the end of the baseboard (where the retaining wall is temporarily positioned) and along the far side.

fencing is available from Peco (LK-744). This can be scribed to represent the sectional concrete fencing adopted by the LMS and BR in later years. Peco also produces a flexible four-bar-style wooden fencing (LK-743) with matching gates, useful for general fencing in the countryside.

Great Western Railway-style 'spear' fencing is available from a number of sources, including two packs of plastic moulded fencing from Peco (LK-741 and LK-742), while Scale Link produces etched-brass spear-point fencing (SLOF01), inclined railings

(SLOF02) and assorted gates (SLOF03). For followers of the Midland Railway, Slater's Plastikard produces diagonal paling (7A13), along with packs of fencing for platform ramps (7A14) and gates (7A15). Although usually associated with the Midland Railway, it is worth noting that this type of fencing was also used by several other railway companies. Slater's also produces packs of thirty-six posts for approximately 3ft (914mm) of 'wooden' fencing (7A10), or concrete post and wire fencing (7A12). There is also a kit for lineside fencing (7A16) and gates (7A17). All

Seen from the other side, blocks of expanded polystyrene are being fixed in position to form the ground dropping away from track level. The ground level will also rise towards the junction, with the main line in the far distance. Using lightweight polystyrene blocks to form the ground surface means that very little weight is carried on the outside of the layout.

A closer view of the coal drops under construction. The piers are blocks of wood cut to fit and clad in Wills 4mm-scale random stone sheet. The white square section styrene tube will form the beams that the rails will rest on – the length of track is a very temporary measure. As two point motors need to be concealed in the coal drops, the top part will be boarded in. The road surface is made up of oddments of Slater's 7mm stonework, while the bases for the piles of coal are cut from high-density foam packaging.

of the above products are produced as either plastic mouldings or in etched-brass, but several manufacturers now offer laser-cut alternatives, for example the 7mm-scale real wood LNWR fence pack from Poppy's WoodTech (PWF7LNWS).

BACK SCENES

The treatment of back scenes is really a matter of personal choice – the back scene on 'Gifford Street' was simply painted to represent a plain pale blue sky with no cloud or other effects. Some choose to add clouds, paint distant scenery, or use photographic back scenes. These days, digital photographs can be stitched together and altered with software such as Adobe Photoshop, then printed out as a banner to provide a seamless backdrop. However, this process can be expensive. Photographic back scenes are also available commercially and the two photographs here illustrate how using this type of back scene can change the appearance of a layout.

Teddy bear fur fabric glued in position over a sub-base of expanded polystyrene forms the ground level in exactly the same way as for the cutting and embankments described earlier.

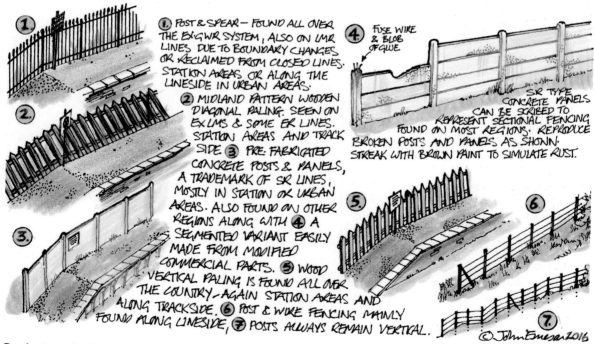

(1.) POST & SPEAR – FOUND ALL OVER THE EX GWR SYSTEM, ALSO ON LMR LINES DUE TO BOUNDARY CHANGES OR RECLAIMED FROM CLOSED LINES. STATION AREAS OR ALONG THE LINESIDE IN URBAN AREAS.

(2) MIDLAND PATTERN WOODEN DIAGONAL PALING. SEEN ON EX LMS & SOME ER LINES. STATION AREAS AND TRACK SIDE (3) PRE-FABRICATED CONCRETE POSTS & PANELS, A TRADEMARK OF SR LINES, MOSTLY IN STATION OR URBAN AREAS. ALSO FOUND ON OTHER REGIONS ALONG WITH (4) A SEGMENTED VARIANT EASILY MADE FROM MODIFIED COMMERCIAL PARTS. (5) WOOD VERTICAL PALING IS FOUND ALL OVER THE COUNTRY – AGAIN STATION AREAS AND ALONG TRACKSIDE. (6) POST & WIRE FENCING MAINLY FOUND ALONG LINESIDE, (7) POSTS ALWAYS REMAIN VERTICAL.

(4.) FUSE WIRE & BLOB OF GLUE

SR TYPE CONCRETE PANELS CAN BE SCRIBED TO REPRESENT SECTIONAL FENCING FOUND ON MOST REGIONS. REPRODUCE BROKEN POSTS AND PANELS AS SHOWN. STREAK WITH BROWN PAINT TO SIMULATE RUST.

© John Emerson 2016

Don't sit on the fence – even in these standardized and privatized times, old company or regional BR identities can still be distinguished by the type of lineside fencing. No need to use unrealistic matchsticks and fluffy cotton thread, as there are plenty of etched frets, plastic mouldings or laser-cut items available. Concrete panel fencing can be easily made from styrene sheet.

Slater's Midland Railway diagonal paling fence (right) was also used by several other railway companies, as was the GWR-style wooden fencing (left). As well as lineside fencing, the post and rail wooden fencing (lower left) found general use as boundaries for agricultural and other land.

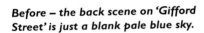

Before – the back scene on 'Gifford Street' is just a blank pale blue sky.

No, not Photoshop – placing a photographic back scene behind the scenery gives apparent extra depth.

MODELLING THE LAZY WAY: TEN IDEAS FOR ARMCHAIR MODELLERS

Not everyone enjoys the delights of scenic modelling, or maybe they just do not have the time or the room for it. When the Manchester to Leeds line was originally built, spoil from the tunnels and cuttings on the line was dumped by the lineside. Over time, this killed off the trees – so I did not have lots of trees to model on 'Gifford Street'! Here are ten more ideas for lazy modellers.

1. Do you really need scenery?

   There are many spectacular scenic layouts around, but it is not essential to model acres of greenery, trees and bushes. In the early days of the hobby layouts consisted mainly of what was on the other side of the railway fence – namely tracks and all the paraphernalia of the railway – with hardly a nod to any scenic work. A fairly simple layout on a narrow baseboard can give just as much enjoyment as a large scenic layout – and in a far shorter time.

2. Back to basics

   Good-quality brick papers and card kits are just as effective as embossed or vacuum-formed plastic. Remember, when viewed from a distance, it is often impossible to see any relief detail such as mortar courses on 12in to the foot buildings – but don't mix and match card kits with plastic, resin and plaster. And there is no need to finish buildings on hidden sides – against back scenes for example – so leave 'em plain.

3. True grit

   A quick and easy way to produce a realistic road surface is to use emery cloth or an aluminium oxide (sand) paper, readily available from DIY stores. Cut to shape with a sharp knife – you will quickly blunt several blades – and stick down with PVA glue, but use a wooden block to smooth down, not your fingers!

4. Paintshop pro

   Prime stone walls, baseboard surfaces and so on with light grey emulsion paint before starting any final painting, weathering or detailing. Emulsion paint gives a good 'ground' for later painting with enamels or acrylics. Do not use lots of different colours, keep to a limited palette – and avoid gloss paints at all costs.

5. Back-scene primer

   Do not be frightened by back scenes – a plain pale blue back scene provides a good foil that won't detract from the rest of the layout. If you paint your own back scene, remember that colour recedes with distance. Watercolours are best – nothing looks worse than a badly painted scene in lurid enamels or oils – but paint in the flat off the layout wherever possible. You can also use photographic back scenes – or create your own on your computer.

6. Get it taped

   Besides its obvious uses, masking tape is great for scenic work. Use it to represent concrete on walls and buildings. It can be layered, painted and stripped back to represent damaged areas on concrete road surfaces. Cover van roofs with masking tape on 7mm-scale rolling stock to represent canvas covering.

7. What a load of ballast

   Ballasting track can make or mar a layout – the colour and type of ballast used will depend on the area and era you are modelling. In general, most proprietary ballasts are way overscale, so use OO-gauge ballast for gauge-O trackwork and fine sand for the cess. Ballast spreaders are now available from several sources to make the job easier – take your time and have a glass of your favourite tipple on hand!

8. Grass cuttings

   Foliage mats provide a quick and effective means of covering large areas and are available in a variety of textures and finishes depicting the seasons of the year. Alternative materials are teddy bear fur fabric, green hanging basket liners and dyed lint – each will give a different texture for different types of grass. Enhance with scatter materials and foliage and disguise edges with static grass.

9. Keep up with the latest products
   The days of brightly dyed sawdust, dried tea leaves and smelly fish glue are long over. Technical innovation means that there are now many new time-saving products on the market – scale trees, grass tufts, laser-cut plant kits, static grass, dedicated adhesives and so on.

Experiment with them, but remember that the hobby does not come ready made in a packet – your skills and abilities will develop with time.

10. Railway modelling is fun!
    Don't take your hobby too seriously – it is meant to be fun and a relaxing way of switching off from everyday life, not a competitive sport. Practice makes perfect, so be prepared to learn from failure or when things go wrong. Record details of how you have produced your scenic work for future reference – you could even write it up for your favourite model railway magazine!

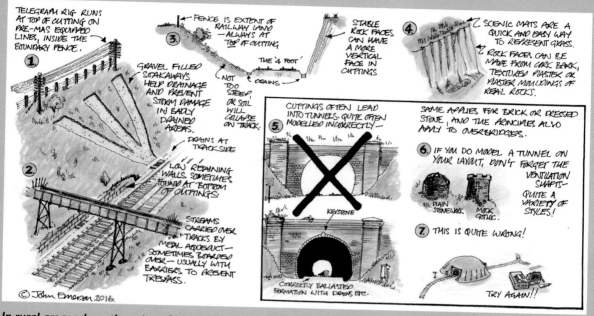

In rural areas where the price of land was not at a premium, railway companies could avoid the great expense of constructing retaining walls and leave shallow sloped sides to cuttings. Retaining walls were only used where the danger of earth slip existed, for example on the approach to tunnels. Tunnels hold their own pitfalls for the unwary modeller – details such as ventilation shafts can help to create atmosphere.

Where tracks run below ground level in urban locations, retaining walls are to be found. Expensive to construct both in materials and manpower, they can pre-date your layout by more than 100 years and often show evidence of later alterations and additions, usually where new roads cross the formation. As always, a little observation of the prototype will pay dividends.

SCENIC SUPPLIERS

Bachmann Europe
Woodland Scenics
www.bachmann.co.uk

Ceynix Railway Trees
Ready-to-plant model trees and tree-building courses
Tel: 020 8864 696
www.railwaytrees.co.uk
email: jacqui@railwaytrees.co.uk

Crossinggate Models
Platform edging kits
Tel: 07709 178381
www.crossinggate.co.uk
email: info@crossinggate.co.uk

Curvilinear By Design
Etched-brass signal box kits
Tel: 01543 254653
www.curvilinear.co.uk
email: mail@curvilinear.co.uk

Duncan Models
Large range of cast accessories
Tel: 01722 321041
www.duncanmodels.co.uk
email: duncan.models@tiscali.co.uk

Finescale Model World
Static grass and applicators, paints and weathering sets
Tel: 01902 650077
www.finescalemodelworld.co.uk
email: finescalemodelrailways@gmail.com

Freestone Model Accessories
Card kits and accessories
Tel: 01993 775979
email: sales@freestonemodel.co.uk

Gaugemaster
Noch scenic materials, back scenes
Tel: 01903 884488
www.gaugemaster.com

Green Scene
Scenic materials
Tel: 01905 24298
email: johns.lloyd@sky.com
www.green-scene.co.uk

Invertrain
Model building kits, accessories, detail parts
Tel: 01383 880844
www.invertrain.com

Langley Models
White-metal road vehicle kits, figures, detail accessories
Tel: 01293 516329
www.langleymodels.co.uk

Lynx Models
White-metal castings, accessories, motorcycle kits
Tel: 01529 469010
www.lynxmodels.net
email: lynxmodels@icloud.com

Model Display Products
Scenic materials
Tel: 07795 957854
www.modeldisplayproducts.co.uk

Omen Miniatures
Scale figures
Tel: 01249 890646
www.omen-miniatures.com
email: nigel@omen-miniatures.com

Peco (Pritchard Patent Product Co. Ltd) including Ratio and Wills
Lineside building and accessory kits, distributed lines
Tel: 01297 21542
www.peco-uk.com

Poppy's Wood Tech
Laser-cut accessories
email: poppys.woodtech@virginmedia.com

Scale Link
Etched-brass detail frets, scenic and architectural items
Tel: 01747 811817
www.scalelink.co.uk
email: info@scalelink.co.uk

Slater's Plastikard
Plastikard, fencing and detail parts
www.slatersplastikard.com

CHAPTER SIX

MODEL BUILDING FOR O GAUGE

GETTING IT RIGHT – EASIER THAN GETTING IT WRONG

CHOOSING A PROTOTYPE AND HOW TO BUILD IT

Along with locomotives, rolling stock and signalling, railway buildings and style of architecture help to identify a region or railway company. So if buildings can make or mar a layout it is worth taking the trouble to get them right in the first place. These days there are plenty of kits, downloads and ready-to-use buildings to take advantage of – O gauge has progressed a long way from the early days of fairly crude wooden buildings covered in shiny brick paper. Building kits are produced in card, plastic, resin and latterly laser-cut from a variety of materials, including card, thin plywood and MDF. There are even etched-brass building kits available, particularly for signal boxes.

Kits, such as the Kittle Hobby footbridge, are excellent subjects for kit-bashing – no kit should ever be finished just as the manufacturer intended! Even if you don't have the confidence to try kit construction, kit-bashing or constructing a building for yourself, there are professional or semi-professional builders who will do it for you.

Overall, there is no 'best' way of making a building; it will come down to the modeller's preference. My own preferred method is laminated styrene sheet and strip – over the years I've tried using card, foam-board, and veneer overlays, but for me nothing seems to work as well or as easily as plastic. But there are those who swear by wood and card, and shun plastic. Others are critical of printed card or paper because there is no depth to the mortar courses on brickwork, although as I look out of the window at the brick-built houses across the way I cannot discern

Almost nothing else more easily identifies a railway company than its buildings. Toddington – on the Gloucestershire, Warwickshire Railway – is typical of Great Western stations built in the early part of the twentieth century. Whilst the station buildings survived into the preservation era, the water tank is new and the footbridge was salvaged from the Midland Railway's High Orchard branch in Gloucester.

any noticeable difference between brick and mortar – they might as well all be built of printed card! In fact, many of the embossed building sheets we use have mortar courses that are way too deep. However, one thing to remember is to avoid mixing buildings made from card, printed card or brick paper with those made from plastic, styrene, resin or cast plaster on the layout. Nothing could look worse, as the eye will always pick up the difference between flat printed surfaces and embossed detail.

Many modellers prefer to take the route of scratchbuilding and this may be the only option for reproducing a particular prototype in miniature. Building from scratch is relatively easy using card, wood or plastic, or a mixture of materials. If you can handle a computer and are comfortable with drawing and 3D modelling software, you can produce your own files for laser-cutting or 3D prototyping. Desktop 3D printers are increasingly becoming a must-have modelling tool, but for the time-being I'll stick with scalpel and straight edge.

Whatever course you choose, a little bit of homework looking at suitable buildings and structures before committing to buying or building will pay dividends. For steam-age modellers, there are plenty of sources of prototype material to provide inspiration, including dedicated books on railway company buildings and the journals and publications of the specialist line societies. DVDs are also a good source of inspiration, as they will give you a glimpse of the 'traditional' railway in operation. For modellers of the contemporary scene, it is not quite a case of just looking over the fence – in these days of heightened security, it is always best to ask first and shoot photographs later.

The larger size of 7mm-scale models means that details are easier to see and consequently easier to add – so in turn it means that they will need to be applied. The unnatural viewpoint on most layouts, where we look down on buildings instead of looking up at them, will only emphasize any missing detail. Fortunately, there are a number of aftermarket suppliers producing 7mm-scale chimneys, window frames, rainwater goods, roof ridges, finials, signal-box fittings, furniture, poster boards, lamps and other detail components, mostly as white-metal or resin castings, or as etched-brass and laser-cut frets to make the job easier.

There is not enough space in this book to feature several pages of 'blow by blow' building articles, so I have instead selected some projects that have featured on my 'Gifford Street' layout that will hopefully show you what can be achieved in 7mm scale and inspire you to have a go. First of all, we'll look at a building that

The signal cabin controlling Calvert Street Crossing on the author's 'Gifford Street' layout. This easy to put together and exceptional value for money kit from Peco is often overlooked by the 'experts', but by taking a little extra time and effort, something out of the ordinary can be produced that will add individuality to your layout.

will benefit from quite a bit of added detail and that almost every layout will need – the signal box.

PECO KIT-BASH

DETAIL YOU CAN SEE

Peco has recently introduced a signal-box kit that is a lovely kit in its own right, does not cost a huge sum of money, is ideal for the smaller layout and can be assembled fairly easily in an evening by modellers of all abilities. It makes a good starting point for someone new to the hobby and that is probably why most modellers may well overlook its potential as a basis for some interesting kit-bashing.

Cutting off a strip of tiles from the roof completely alters the look of the Peco signal box. Use a sharp

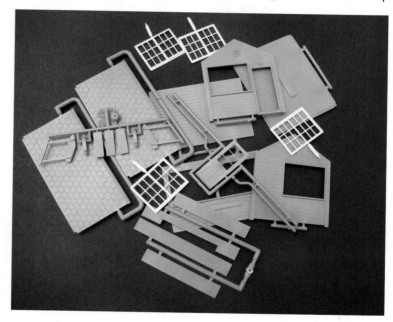

RIGHT: *What you get in the Peco signal-box kit: a bag full of dark-grey injection-moulded plastic for the base, walls and roof; window mouldings in white plastic; and glazing. A set of clear illustrated instructions completes the kit.*

A 'dry run' (and some sticky tape) shows you what the kit is supposed to build up into – an attractive small signal box that will look exactly the same as everyone else's Peco signal box! But that roof overhang worries me.

Assembling the kit is a fairly easy affair, ensuring that everything fits together well and is square. The addition of interior detail will help to give the box an identity – I used the white metal Springside interior kit, although strictly speaking this is designed for Great Western signal boxes.

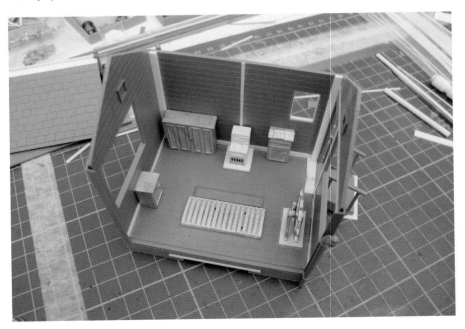

Construction lends itself to the front wall being removable – at least until the final painting stage – which is handy for placing lever frame and other details such as styrene-strip corner posts and skirting. A window aperture has also been cut into the rear wall as this is a gate box, so the 'bobby' will want to observe road traffic before closing the gates.

With basic construction complete, interior installed and painting in progress, it is time for a glass of something over the Christmas holiday. Metallic foil off the bottle top is a useful modelling material – some of it will be shaped to form the signalman's coat hanging on the wall. Who says railway modelling should be a serious affair? Cheers!

Now we're getting there – with the front wall removed and interior painted, apart from the levers, you can see the asbestos sheet placed between the stove and the timber wall to prevent the signal box catching fire! The fire extinguisher is probably a bit too modern and should really be one of the older conical-shaped type.

knife against a steel straight edge and cut from the back (plain) side – if you don't, the knife blade will make an erratic cut as it tries to follow the line of the tiles. When the cut is deep enough, snap the excess material off. The roof can then be made good with styrene strip. Ridge tiles are also made from the same material, rounded off with a file and scribed to represent individual tiles. With the roof and finials assembled, new styrene strip bargeboards can be added to hide any mismatch where the roof has been cut.

With the altered roof and base covered with Slater's brick-embossed Plastikard, the look of the Peco signal box has been completely changed. The fire buckets were drilled out and fitted with wire spigots glued into holes drilled into the side of the signal box for added strength – do not rely on just gluing the handles, as the buckets will eventually fall off!

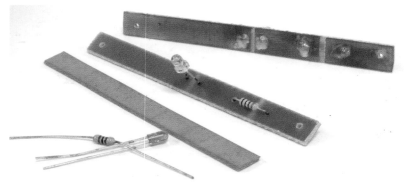

A simple lighting unit was made up from a piece of PCB strip to hold the LED and current limiting resistor, which is then concealed under the roof. On no account should the LED be fed directly with 12V DC.

The lighting unit on the finished model will be soldered to two concealed brass rods running down the inside of the front corner posts, through the baseboard and connected to the 12V DC power supply. The interior detail shows up nicely, including the signalman's coat now hanging on the left-hand wall made from folded metallic foil.

The completed signal box installed at Calvert Street Crossing on 'Gifford Street', with the 'bobby' visible through the window writing up the train register. For a small outlay and a modest amount of additional work, the Peco signal-box kit builds up into a splendid model, which will add a little individuality to even the smallest layout.

Another view of the completed signal box at Calvert Street Crossing – its small size makes it ideal for use as a crossing keeper's box, or in confined locations, or for industrial use or engine sheds. But why stop there?

CROSSING THE LINE: BLACK BULL CROSSING

An assembly line of signal boxes, all bashed from the Peco kit. To alter the appearance radically, a porch can be added, a relatively simple scratch-building exercise for which I used Evergreen styrene sheet and strip.

Adding a porch raises the game – although fitting it to the other end of the signal box as here really was a step too far and is not to be recommended. The kit would also benefit from the addition of a chimney – humble stovepipe or brick stack – which again lifts the model into a different league.

Rear view of the much modified Peco signal box showing the amount of added brickwork that would in reality include a corner fireplace and support the weight of the chimney stack. At the porch end, the position of the doorway had to be swapped over and the width of the windows reduced by one pane to give a 2+3 arrangement.

The much modified signal box is destined for Black Bull Crossing on 'Gifford Street' – the level crossing is another excellent Peco product, which will also benefit from some extra work and detail. First, the road surface had to be built up from offcuts of plywood so that it was approximately at rail level (but no higher). The road surface will be added later.

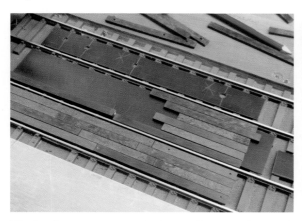

The level crossing conceals the join between flat-bottom and bullhead rail on the main line. Strips of black plastic were first cut to the width of the roadway and glued between the rails – holes were drilled to allow for any track pins standing proud that might prevent the timbers forming the crossing surface from lying flat.

C&L plastic point timbering was used for the crossing surface, drilled, countersunk and pinned with track pins to represent bolt fixings. Lengths of various sizes were selected and tried in different combinations to ensure that all joints were staggered. The surface was then sanded and edges between the running rails rounded off.

Out of the box – component parts of the Peco Level Crossing kit are cleanly moulded in white plastic, obviating the need for painting, although they will benefit from a coat of white primer from a 'rattle can'. The only alterations were to drill out the lamps to take red brilliants and replace the plastic supporting rods with brass wire.

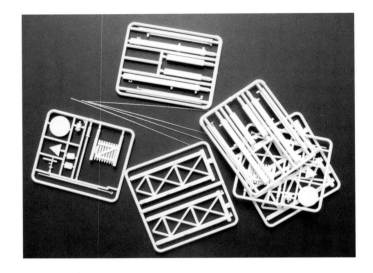

The level-crossing gates assembled and test-fitted. The kit appears to be based on a prototype with concrete posts for the main gates, so these were painted a light-grey colour and suitably weathered. The wicket gates should always be positioned so that they open away from the railway – leave plenty of room between gates and passing trains, too. The gates are correctly detailed for hand operation, so would need altering to represent gates operated by a gate wheel in the cabin.

'The Black Bull' pub, originally built some years ago by Allan Downes. Several of Allan's buildings grace the layout, all substantially constructed from reinforced card. This produced surprisingly strong structures, as we discovered when trying to butcher a factory building with a large panel saw to make it fit snugly into its new home.

SIGNAL-BOX SCRATCH-BUILD

WHEN KITS ARE NOT ENOUGH

For the main line, something larger than the Peco signal box is needed and although some kits are available, often the only recourse is to scratch-build. Signal boxes pose a problem because the large area of glazing required can result in a fairly weak structure. These two signal boxes on 'Gifford Street' were both built from scratch using laminated sheet styrene. The later LMR Type 15 box was built as three separate parts – brick base, upper cabin and the roof. The base and cabin were joined together when complete, but the roof remains removable for fitting the interior. The

large all-wooden L&Y signal box is also constructed from laminated sheet styrene, clad in Evergreen strip to represent the style of planking used by the L&Y, but built as two units – the box and the roof. In both models the glazing used is a fairly thick material for rigidity, overlaid with styrene strip for glazing bars.

The steps for both models were constructed from styrene, the LMR Type 15 having tubular metal rails soldered up from brass wire in a simple jig. Both were time-consuming but satisfying models to build, although I'm sorry to say that after many years on 'Gifford Street' and its predecessor 'Utterly', the L&Y signal box still waits patiently to have its guttering and downpipes fitted. One day!

The L&Y timber signal box at 'Gifford Street', scratch-built from styrene sheet overlaid with Evergreen styrene 'planking'. The laser-cut roof tiles are from York Modelmaking, with ridge tiles built up from styrene strip. The Up home signal – illuminated with an LED and worked by a simple 'memory wire' motor built by Mick Nicholson – is one of the excellent Midland Railway Centre kits, sadly no longer available. TONY WRIGHT, COURTESY BRITISH RAILWAY MODELLING

A closer look at the laser-cut tiling on the roof – I like the slight brown burn marks around the cuts, which give an impression of well-worn weathering without the need for further painting. Full interior detail and lighting have been installed, but guttering and downpipes are still missing after many years of service on the layout – the signalman started life as a Peco civilian.

Do not forget the clutter associated with running a full-size railway when detailing your layout. The 'bobby's' scooter rests safely by the coal bin – shades of **The Love Match** starring Arthur Askey and Glenn Melvyn – but how that saw is balanced on the saw bench is a complete mystery.

A rear view of the LMR Type 15 signal box amidst the chaos of rebuilding the yards at the rear of 'Gifford Street'. It was built as separate base, cabin and roof units, again from laminated styrene sheet. The stairway had been removed for safety while work progressed on the layout.

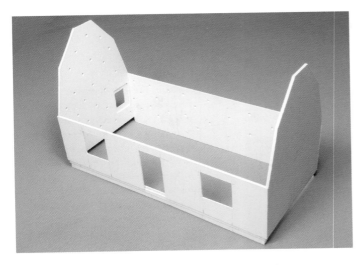

Scratch-building in styrene is quite an easy process, as demonstrated by Paul Bason. This carcass for a 7mm-scale thatched cottage is made from laminated sheet styrene – apertures for doors and windows are larger on the inside to facilitate glazing. Holes drilled in the interior walls allow solvent to be applied. *PAUL BASON*

The completed cottage.
PAUL BASON

PAINTING BY NUMBERS

GETTING THE BEST FROM SKYTREX FLATS

Most layouts will have some sort of back scene to hide tools, mugs, assorted clutter and quite often oversized stomachs! Back scenes can range from plain blue or cloudy sky to detailed painted and photographic scenes. On 'Gifford Street', a large area of bland blue sky existed behind the 10ft (3m) or so of siding in the goods yard that needed disguising. Fortunately, Skytrex produces a useful range of resin-cast low-relief buildings, including factory sections with northlight roof in four-window/two-bay modules with downpipes and so on. These flats cover a variety of residential and industrial subjects as well as brick arches, typical of the approaches to towns and cities where the railway is often elevated above street level.

Most layouts have a back scene of sorts and low-relief buildings can be a great way to add interest to a scene. This low-relief factory made from Skytrex 'flats' provides an industrial backdrop to shunting operations on 'Gifford Street' and took a lot less time to install than building a similar structure from scratch.

The industrial flats can be divided into three basic groups:

- stone buildings – typical of much older structures
- more modern types – including examples from the 1940s and 1990s
- brick-built – with northlight roof.

The latter group forms the basis of a large low-relief factory on 'Gifford Street'. Five single-storey brick two-bay units with northlight (SMRS37) were acquired, along with a single-storey brick single bay with loading bay (SMRS37B) and interior kit (SMRS37C), although in the event the interior kit was not used. These modules are also all available in two-storey form, which look even more impressive!

The components require a degree of cleaning up before construction can begin – although there was no distortion, blow holes or other casting defects to be filled in, the windows had a considerable amount of flash over the rather delicate glazing bars that had to be removed with care. I used a sharp scal-

A low-relief resin casting before cleaning up for painting and detailing.

pel to pare away the excess, then ran a file around the inside of the window bars. As the castings varied slightly in thickness, the back of the thicker castings was rubbed down on coarse emery paper. The best method is to glue a sheet of emery paper to a flat surface such as a piece of board, then gently move the casting around in a circular motion, sanding the rear face until a smooth, even finish is achieved. The edges were also dressed with a large coarse file so that the various sections fitted together more closely – part of the roof at one side was also filed back to achieve a good fit when fixing castings together.

Before painting, wash the castings in warm soapy water to get rid of any greasy fingerprints, release agent and so on, then leave to dry thoroughly. The castings were then given an all-over even base coat of Halford's Red Oxide acrylic spray primer and again left to dry thoroughly. Although the Red Oxide colour is much too strong, it will assume a more natural appearance once it is weathered down. All further painting and weathering was carried out using matt enamel paint from the Humbrol and Precision ranges, although you may prefer to use acrylics.

First, the area between the windows, from the sill to the base of the window arch, was painted to form a light-coloured band using matt Humbrol No.28. Plenty of time was allowed for the paint to dry thoroughly before the brickwork received attention using Humbrol Nos 28 and 29 dry-brushed across the brick courses. Brush the paint on using diagonal strokes to give an uneven effect, then highlight by separately dry-brushing a mix of Nos 28 and 29 on to the brickwork. The circular ventilators and window arches were picked out in Engineers Blue Brick (Precision P954) and the stone sills painted with Humbrol No.28, knocked back with a touch of Humbrol 29. Finally, the coping stones on the roof were painted with the same mix. When the paint had completely dried, further dry-brushing was used to produce vertical streaking on the brickwork beneath the sills and coping stones. This effectively finished the main part of the painting, so the next step was to add the lettering, glaze the windows and secure the low-relief castings to the back scene.

The area between the window sill and bottom of the arch was painted in a light off-white/cream colour to contrast with the lettering of the company name.

Before applying the lettering, a rough sketch was made to position and space the lettering correctly. I used some old dry-print rub-down lettering – not a style that I really wanted, but as it was the right size it was a case of 'make do'. A base line was pencilled in along one of the brick courses and the lettering carefully lined up and applied by rubbing down with an old ballpoint pen. With the lettering complete, the backing sheet was placed over the dry transfer characters and rubbed down again to ensure that they had firmly adhered to the brickwork. The lettering was then 'distressed' by dry-brushing Humbrol No.28 over the top of the black characters to give the effect of brickwork showing through worn paint. An alternative method would be to draw out the lettering on thin card or thickish paper and cut a stencil. Paint can then be stippled through the stencil and the lettering tidied up afterwards.

I used some fairly poor-quality clear plastic mouldings from inexpensive plastic building kits as glazing. As there is no interior there was no need for top-quality crystal-clear glazing. These were attached to the cleaned up backs of the castings with impact adhesive. As the glazing adds some extra depth to the

The join between the two factory modules in the centre of the picture is effectively masked by the rainwater hopper and downpipe. Using poor-quality moulded glazing from a cheap building kit helps to hide the fact that there is no interior behind those windows – it would be possible to arrange the windows with some of the fanlights opened, although for simplicity I left them as closed.

castings, a card sub-base was then glued to the back scene with impact adhesive and that part of the back scene visible behind the windows was painted matt black. The painted castings were then fixed in position on the back scene and sub-base, ensuring that they were all level and adjusting any difference in the thickness of the castings. It would be entirely possible to drill fixing holes in the castings, countersink them and screw in place on the back scene, although the fixing points would need to be disguised afterwards. Once happy with the position and fixing, it was a simple matter of final detailing, touching up the paintwork and weathering where necessary.

Detailing consisted of adding the resin-cast downpipes after priming and painting, along with a lamp or two and a wall-mounted telephone box. The downpipes were carefully positioned over the joins between the castings, effectively helping to conceal them. The flood lamp is a non-working Eckon 4mm-scale casting attached with impact adhesive. Finally, a little foliage was added to conceal any gaps between the bottom of the castings and ground level. The only other work carried out was the construction of some plain northlight wall sections from laminated sheet plastic and embossed brickwork to echo the style of the resin castings. These were positioned at either end of the resin-cast factory.

The result is a quite convincing large factory, typical of those seen by the lineside in urban areas and equally at home on steam- or diesel-era layouts, but conveniently produced in a fraction of the time it would have taken to scratch-build a similar structure.

Not a lot of room. This view looking back along the siding at the rear of the goods yard shows the narrow, low-relief nature of these resin castings – ideal against back scenes, they can be used just about anywhere.

Looking across the goods yard with the low-relief factory as a backdrop. The car sales signage is taken from a dealer in 1960s Birmingham, using suitably distressed Letraset dry-print transfers – in 1962 a second-hand Ford Popular 100E would set you back around £200–300, while a brand-new Ford Zodiac Mk III cost £1,070.

The view from ground level – any unwanted gaps between the bottom of the Skytrex low-relief building and the baseboard were covered with scenic dressing.

The completed low-relief factory in position against the plain back scene of one of the goods yard boards. The Provender Store is scratch-built and the aggregate hopper is another kit-bash, this time using the 4mm-scale Ratio Coal Hopper as detailed below.

The Provender Store, a typical railway structure scratch-built in styrene sheet from plans published by the LMS Society in Model Railways *back in the 1970s, although at least two versions are now available ready-to-use cast in resin. During construction, a dimensional error was discovered on the plan – so measure twice and cut once!*

INDUSTRIAL ACTION – COAL-HOPPER CONVERSIONS

Prototype inspiration at Tallington – much too large for 'Gifford Street', but providing the initial germ of an idea for the smaller aggregate hopper on the layout. 'Observe the prototype' is a good maxim for modellers.

The basis of the hopper is a Ratio 4mm-scale kit – never underestimate what the O-gauge modeller can beg, steal or borrow from other scales or modelling disciplines! The height has been extended with styrene sheet and strip in the style of the donor kit to disguise its smaller-scale origins – the cut-out on the right is for the loading conveyor.

Virtually complete apart from the handrails around the top platform. The turned-brass handrail stanchions are designed for model ships – raiding other modelling disciplines again – the concrete fence is simply made from scribed styrene sheet. Hacked-up offcuts of poystyrene insulation form the basic shape for the pile of aggregate.

Complete with handrails installed and added details, including water tap, control box, conduit for electric light and conveyor, plus working floodlight (from 4mm-scale Eckon range). The typical rail-side concrete fencing is simply made from scribed Plastikard, with thicker material overlaid for the posts.

Another view of the completed hopper. The original intention was to model the (non-working) conveyor belt complete with scratch-built gantry and rollers using old typewriter ribbon for the belt, but lack of time forced a simpler solution. The concrete areas were simply made from 4in decorator's masking tape, suitably painted and weathered.

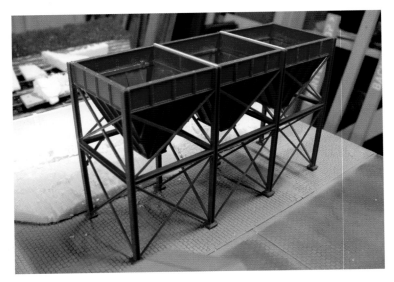

Flushed with success after building the aggregate hopper, thoughts turned to creating a set of hoppers for a Coal Concentration Depot. This used three Ratio 4mm Coal Hopper kits as a basis, one built up as per the instructions, with the other two added on either side.

The tops of the hoppers were built up with styrene sheet on three sides in a different style to the aggregate hopper. The structure was then clad in Wills 4mm-scale Corrugated Asbestos Sheet before spraying the entire structure in Halford's grey acrylic primer. Blocks of black foam form the basis for adding a graded coal load.

The front of the finished Coal Concentration Depot hopper. Although the intention was to add the weighing and bagging machinery on the loading platform, it was left off after the model was completed when it was discovered that there was not enough room for the coal depot on the layout – there is a moral in there somewhere!

ON THE BUSES – CORRUGATED CONVERSATIONS

Calvert Street bus garage is a simple plywood box clad in brick-embossed Plastikard and Wills 4mm-scale corrugated sheet. The top of the diesel tank – also a 4mm kit – is just visible and the Burlingham Seagull coaches in Yelloways livery parked up in the garage yard are Corgi diecasts.

Lighting conduit is plastic rod of various diameters, the ventilator is left over from an LMS van kit, the water tap is a white-metal casting and the door was scrounged from the 'spares' box (which all aspiring modellers should have). Lettering is ancient and distressed Letraset and a working Eckon 4mm floodlight completes the detailing.

The hidden secrets of the bus garage are revealed – plywood walls and MDF roof, all glued and screwed and put together without a lot of care, but well braced to avoid warping. The wiring is for the working light and the cut-out at the rear is to allow access to switches controlling lighting and so on.

Prototype inspiration for the bus garage came from this now demolished garage premises photographed in Bourne, Lincolnshire. Several digital photographs were taken and used as a guide for painting and weathering.

More hidden secrets of the bus garage – as the Corgi vehicles are to the smaller 1:50 scale, the garage yard was raised up on ½in MDF, the difference in height being concealed by a tall fence. This helped to create the impression that the coaches were much larger and to the same scale as the 1:43-scale vehicles in the surrounding streets.

PROTOTYPE INSPIRATION – JUST THE REAL THING

The signal box at Wansford on the present-day Nene Valley Railway typifies LNWR practice of timber cabin on a solid brick base. Note that part of the lower rear wall is angled with the cabin overhanging. There is also some useful detail for modellers in the deck of the bridge spanning the River Nene.

The Midland favoured a delicate style of glazed canopy as here at Cheltenham Lansdown, on the Bristol to Birmingham route. BR Standard 5MT 4-6-0 No.73040 runs into the station with a southbound train.
THE LATE ROY TAYLOR/JOHN EMERSON COLLECTION

Rippingale on the Great Northern Railway's line between Bourne and Sleaford dates from 1872 and was closed to passengers as long ago as 1930, although the section from Bourne to Billingborough remained open to goods traffic until 1964. The old station has been sympathetically restored as a private dwelling, complete with length of railway track and the odd loco or two.

Highley Station opened in 1862 on the Severn Valley Railway, later absorbed into the Great Western Railway and finally closed in 1963. Fortunately, the buildings survived into preservation to become part of the new Severn Valley Railway, reopening in 1974.

The abandoned Withington signal box on the M&SWJR line between Andoversford Junction and Swindon Town – something similar could be kit-bashed from the Peco kit.

ROY TAYLOR/JOHN EMERSON COLLECTION

Highley signal box on the Severn Valley Railway is a larger structure, but would also make a good prototype for a model signal box.

GETTING THAT LINESIDE LOOK

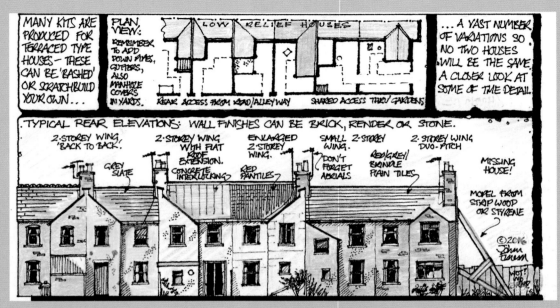

The great outback – terraced houses have been a common sight from the train since the beginning of the railway age. Although various kits, downloads and ready-to-use buildings are available to make a fine backdrop to your layout, it's worth a look in some detail to get it right, especially if adding terraced houses to a modern period layout where there will have been alterations and additions over the years.

The roofline of terrace houses reveal differences in the construction and finish of chimney stacks – brick and render, round and square pots seen on the same stack, etc. Modern practice is to remove or reduce the height of the stack, and cap it with a metal vent – usually where central heating has been installed. Plenty of scope for detailing here! Thanks to Harvey Faulkner-Aston for supplying notes and details.

Duncan Models
Large range of cast accessories
Tel: 01722 321041
www.duncanmodels.co.uk
email: duncan.models@tiscali.co.uk

Freestone Model Accessories
Card kits including Prototype Models, Howard Scenics, Alphagraphix
Tel: 01993 775979
www.freestonemodel.co.uk
email: sales@freestonemodel.co.uk

Kirtley Model Buildings
Commission-built layouts, buildings, structures and accessories
Tel: 01664 857805
www.kirtleymodels.com
email: kirtleymodels@ntlworld.com

Kittle Hobby
Heljan/Kittle Hobby footbridge and signal box kits
Tel: 01639 731005
www.kittlehobby.com
email: banksofkittle@aol.com

Laira 83D Models
O-gauge buildings
Tel: 01664 567703
email: lairamodels021@gmail.com

Langley Models
White-metal road vehicle kits, figures, detail accessories
Tel: 01293 516329
www.langleymodels.co.uk

Lynx Models
White-metal castings, accessories, model building, weathering services
Tel: 01529 469010
www.lynxmodels.net
email: lynxmodels@icloud.com

Peco (Pritchard Patent Product Co. Ltd)
Track, points, Setrack, lineside building and accessory kits, distributed lines
Tel: 01297 21542
www.peco-uk.com

Phoenix Precision Paints
Churchward Models etched-brass signal box and footbridge kits
Tel: 01268 730549
www.phoenixpaints.co.uk

PLM Cast-A-Ways
Figures and accessories
Tel: 01902 339011

Port Wynnstay Models
Standard- and narrow-gauge kits, tram parts, architectural components
www.portwynnstay.co.uk
email: phil@portwynnstay.co.uk

Rail Model
Laser Craft Devon range of laser-cut building kits and etched signal kits
www.railmodel.co.uk
email: salesrailmodel@gmail.com

Scale Link
Etched-brass detail frets, scenic and architectural items
Tel: 01747 811817
www.scalelink.co.uk
email: info@scalelink.co.uk

Skytrex (2013)
Resin-cast building kits, low-relief buildings, accessories
Tel: 01509 213789
www.skytrex.com
email: sales@skytrex.com

continued overleaf

LIST OF SUPPLIERS *continued*

Springside Models
Cast white-metal loco kits and detail parts
Tel: 01803 813749
www.springsidemodels.com
email: springsidemodels@btinternet.com

Streetscene Models
Hand-built buildings
Tel: 07470 11707
www.streetscenemodels.co.uk
email: pauld.davenport@btinternet.com

Timber Tracks
Laser-cut building kits, accessories, building service
Tel: 01275 852027
www.timbertracks.co.uk
email: sales@timbertracks.co.uk

Townstreet
Stone-cast building kits
Tel: 01768 88456

York Modelmaking and Display Ltd
Laser-cut building kits, accessories, laser-cutting service
Tel: 0194 400358
www.yorkmodelmaking.com
email: info@yorkmodelmaking.com

CHAPTER SEVEN

TAKING STOCK

CHOOSING LOCOS, COACHES AND WAGONS

Unlike modellers starting out in OO or N gauge, the O-gauge modeller does not have the option of a RTR train set or train packs to fall back on as a starting point. Consequently, locomotives and rolling stock will have to be acquired from a variety of different suppliers and manufacturers from day one. The likelihood is that the majority of rolling stock on O-gauge layouts will be built from kits – in other words, indulging in real modelling. If you are moving up from the smaller scales and are well versed in kit construction, this probably will not pose any problems – buying one or two wagon kits and assembling them will provide an enjoyable few hours, boost your confidence and give you a feel for the scale. Then, if you decide that O gauge really is not for you after all, you will not have wasted a great deal of time or money and will at least have a nice model to keep on the mantelpiece or to

sell on. However, it's a fairly safe bet that having built at least one O-gauge model, you will become acutely aware that the O-gauge bug has bitten! One of the first things you will notice is that O-gauge models, being larger, have more mass and roll more easily than models in the smaller scales. Adding detail is easier and when complete you end up with much more model for your money.

However, locomotives are a different matter. Unless building something like a simple starter kit (the Andrew Barclay 0-4-0ST or Class 02 diesel shunter available from Tower Models, for example), the average beginner may well find most locomotive kits far too complex for a first-time build and be put off from further attempts at O-gauge modelling. However, with an increasing number of relatively inexpensive small tank locos now available, a more likely first step for the aspiring twenty-first century O-gauge modeller will be to acquire one of the recent RTR models – something like Dapol's

Fowler 4F 0-6-0 No.43940 and an unidentified 'Compound' 4-4-0 make a spirited departure from Cheltenham Lansdown station with a northbound train in the 1950s. The 4F is lamped for a 'stopper', suggesting that this may be a local service, with the 4F working back north to save a path for a Light Engine working, not uncommon on the Bristol–Birmingham line. Recreating a scene like this in O gauge will require a lot of kit-building.

JOHN EMERSON COLLECTION

One of the latest generation of RTR O-gauge locomotives, a Minerva Models 'E' Class Peckett 0-4-0ST. A small locomotive like this makes a realistically priced first loco for those moving into O-gauge modelling.
COURTESY CHRIS KLEIN, MINERVA MODELS

exceptionally popular 'Terrier', for example, is ideal for a small starter layout.

Starting off with an RTR loco actually has many benefits – you don't have to spend time building it, plus you will have a reliable piece of motive power without the worry of having to make it actually work and so will be able to get a layout up and running in a reasonably short amount of time. You can then spend more time on building up a collection of rolling stock. Far better to start off with an RTR loco and improve your modelling skills building freight rolling stock before moving on to locomotive and passenger carriage kits.

FREIGHT STOCK

One of the greatest revolutions in 7mm scale has been the introduction of high-quality injection-moulded plastic kits for items of freight rolling stock, bringing practical rolling-stock construction within the reach of almost everyone and to standards enjoyed previously only by 4mm-scale modellers. Two names stand out, Parkside Dundas and Slater's, both offering a large range of pre-Grouping, 'Big Four' and British Railways freight stock (plus coaches and parcel vans in the case of Slater's). The kits from these ranges will also be complete – that is, wheels and couplings are included (as well as transfers in the case

The contents of a typical injection-moulded plastic kit – this is the Parkside Dundas GWR 'Tevan' (PS48), which is supplied complete with wheels, couplings and transfers for GWR and BR periods. The main components are finely detailed plastic mouldings with etched-brass frets for the fold-up steps and gedge (coupling) hooks. Kits like these make ideal entry-level projects for those wanting to move up to O gauge.

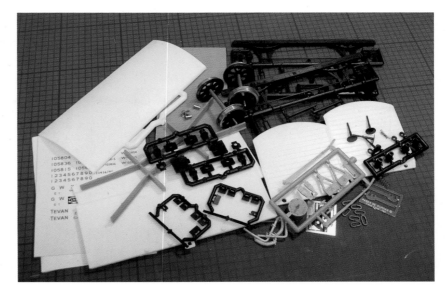

of Parkside and Peco). Almost as easy to assemble as an old-style Airfix construction kit, anyone used to this kind of kit-building can, with a little patience, build a splendid piece of rolling stock over a period of a couple of evenings or so. An open or mineral wagon makes a good starting point for the newcomer, as most layouts will need more than one, and suitable kits are readily available from model shops, at shows, or by mail order.

The majority of these kits require no soldering whatsoever, so only a basic tool kit is needed: a scalpel or a modelling knife with straight and curved blades for cutting and scraping is an essential; a pair of side cutters (Tamiya or Xuron for example) for cutting plastic sprue without damaging the components is more of a luxury (a razor saw is an alternative); small engineer's set square; small Swiss files or emery boards for sanding; a suitable plastic solvent such as MekPak, PlasticWeld or Plastic Magic; and brushes for applying solvent and painting. A piece of plate glass is an essential piece of workbench equipment – you will need this to place the model on from time to time to check that all the wheels are level. At a pinch, a small mirror tile will do.

Some kits, particularly in the Slater's range, include etched-brass components and these give a useful introduction to working with metal for the novice. If you are feeling slightly more adventurous, there are plenty of white-metal and etched-brass kits available from the likes of ABS, Connoisseur, Haywood, Scorpio and WEP. The etched kit is probably the oldest type, with a history going back to the pioneering days

of Sayer-Chaplin 4mm-scale parts produced in the 1940s and 1950s. Over time, the photo-etching process has improved – early kits had hand-drawn artwork, but now the majority use some form of CAD software and quite sophisticated kits are produced in brass or nickel silver, which is better for soldering. Most etched kits also make good use of 'slot and tab' construction, which makes assembly easier – kits such as those in the Connoisseur 'Skill-builder' series can make an ideal starting point for those who may not be confident of their soldering skills, so have not built an etched kit before.

Almost as old as etched kits, white metal became a popular material through the 1960s, as 4mm manufacturers such as Ken Keyser and Robert Wills began to introduce locomotive and rolling stock kits. Whilst easy to build using adhesive or low-melt solder and temperature-controlled soldering iron, the result can be a pretty hefty item of stock, ideal for locomotives where additional weight is often needed to give adequate traction, but the weight of freight rolling stock can affect the length of train a loco can haul if all the wagons consist of white metal only. A lot of white-metal kits now include components in other materials, including etched metal, lost-wax brass castings, resin and so on, whilst some manufacturers are replacing white-metal components with resin-cast parts.

Kits that have a combination of several types of materials (most often resin, plastic, white metal and etched-brass) are commonly referred to as mixed-media kits. A relatively early exponent of mixed-

Rolling stock built from injection-moulded plastic kits can save a considerable amount of time and result in highly detailed and authentic models – many also make suitable subjects for kit-bashing.

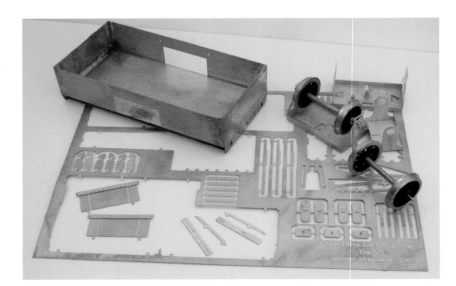

Erecting an etched-brass wagon kit – this is a GWR 10 ton Loco coal wagon from Warren Shephard's range.

The completed GWR loco coal wagon finished in weathered GWR freight-grey livery – a piece of scrap foam packaging has been shaped to form the base for the coal load.

Etched-brass brake vans often suffer from a 'tinplate toy' look unless the exposed edges of the brass sheet on verandah ends is thickened up – this RJH 'Shark' ballast plough has had additional thickening pieces added to the verandah and corner pillars, resulting in a much more solid-looking model.

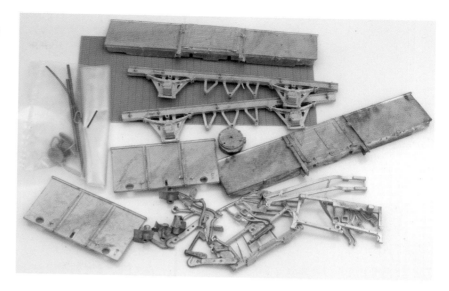

The contents of a typical white-metal freight stock kit – an LNER 13T steel open from the ABS range. The floor is a simple embossed styrene insert.

media kits was Frank Titcombe's Freightman range, using home-grown injection-moulded parts for the van body and ABS white-metal underframe components. Contemporary sources include Appleby Model Engineering (resin, etched-brass and white metal), CRT and Just Like The Real Thing (resin/plastic body components with etched-brass underframes and white-metal or lost-wax brass castings for details). Unlike most injection-moulded plastic kits, mixed-

media kits will probably need wheels to be purchased separately (although wagon kits from JLTRT include wheels), so check with the supplier or manufacturer before purchasing.

READY-TO-RUN

Whilst kit building will probably appeal to most modellers changing to 7mm scale, there will also be those who, for whatever reason, have little or no interest

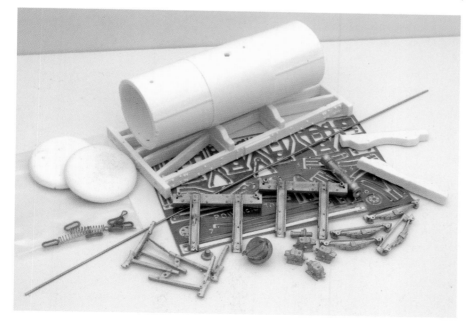

A CRT Sulphuric Acid tank wagon, typical of mixed-media kits containing a mixture of resin, cast white metal and etched-brass components.

The ex-RJH/W&CW kit for the TTB Monobic tank wagon (now available from PR Model Railway Products) builds into a typical convincing but 'generic' vehicle. The kit can be considered mixed media, consisting of aluminium tank barrel, turned aluminium ends, etched-brass underframe and ladder, plus cast white-metal buffers and details.

in kits and choose the RTR route. Although the available range of RTR O-gauge freight stock is unlikely to match what is produced for the 4mm- and N-gauge modeller, nevertheless a good basic range is being established for those who either do not want to build their own stock, or see RTR as a useful adjunct to their own stock-building programme. There is also

the fact that RTR models can save valuable modelling time, which can then be used for other projects. Thanks to the efforts of Dapol, Heljan and Lionheart Trains, the range of O-gauge RTR freight stock is steadily expanding. To date, BR mineral wagons, private-owner coal and coke wagons, various tank wagons, an SR 'Pill Box' brake van and modern air-braked

KIT-BUILT FREIGHT STOCK

BR fitted/unfitted stock	ABS, Connoisseur Models, JLTRT, M&M Models, Modern Motive Power, Parkside, Peco, Slater's
56T Tyne Dock iron ore	Signature Models
BR air-braked stock	Appleby Model Engineering, Buzz Models, GH Plant, Modern Motive Power, PR Model Railway Products
GWR	ABS, Connoisseur Models, Haywood Railway, Parkside, Peco, Scorpio, Slater's (ex-Coopercraft), WEP
LMS	ABS, Haywood Railway, Modern Motive Power, Parkside, Slater's
LNER	ABS, Connoisseur Models, Haywood Railway, Parkside, Slater's
SR	ABS, Haywood Railway, Parkside, Roxey Mouldings
Private Owner	ABS, Haywood Railway, Parkside, Slater's
Tank wagons	CRT, Modern Motive Power, PR Model Railway Products, Slater's (including rectangular tar tank)
Miscellaneous	Peter Clark (Plasseur & Thueurer Tamper, Windhoff MPV)

Development of RTR freight stock – Skytrex 'Suncole' eight-plank coke wagon, Dapol eight-plank Private Owner and Lionheart BR 16T mineral wagon.

Heljan 22T Class B tank wagon in Regent livery.

Latest from Lionheart Trains – 14T ex-Air Ministry tank wagons in a variety of liveries for Class A and Class B products. This is one of a pair custom-weathered for a customer.

four-wheel and bogie stock have become available. Further developments will see Dapol introducing BR standard 12T vans and a 13T open wagon with a similar specification to the Lionheart range, including a compensating beam underframe. Later releases will include air-braked HAA and HEA hopper wagons to accompany the Class 08 diesel shunter.

KIT – OR BUILD FROM SCRATCH?

However, where a kit or RTR vehicle is not available, scratch-building (or a long wait) are the only options. Building from scratch is not as difficult as it first sounds, especially using easily available modern styrene sheet, strip and rod material. Scratch-building in sheet metal

will require some extra skill, but again is not overly difficult for a modeller with some experience. In many cases, scratch-building is merely a natural progression from kit-bashing, or where kit components need to be replaced for whatever reason.

Start with a simple project such as a container or body for a wagon or van before moving on to more complicated prototypes. There are also plenty of ready-made components and fittings such as buffers, axle guards, axle boxes, roof vents and so on to make construction easier. As with all things, be prepared for the odd failure – remember we only learn from our mistakes – and your skills will improve with experience.

Kit-bash, scratch-build, or ready-to-run? Scratch-built demountable road tank on six-wheel GWR 'Rotank' carrier wagon built using modified Slater's components – part of a small batch of models produced by Michelle Davison some years ago.

This six-wheel LMS milk van by Andrew Baldwin has scratch-built sides, but uses commercial parts for the roof, modified ends, axle guards, axle boxes and springs, brake-lever guide and buffers to produce another out of the ordinary vehicle.

COACHING AND MULTIPLE-UNIT STOCK

The development of O-gauge coaching stock is broadly similar to freight stock. Most kits will usually fall into the mixed-media category, having a mixture of etched-brass body and underframe components, with white-metal or lost-wax brass detail castings. Those in the Westdale range make use of pre-formed aluminium bodyshells with punched-out windows, an MDF floor and a combination of white-metal, lost-wax brass or resin castings for detail parts. BR Mk2

coach and DMU kits also include etched-brass frets for roof detail. Far from being old-fashioned or out-moded technology, they make a good entry point for those moving up to O gauge, whilst for the more experienced modeller, or those who enjoy adding their own level of detail, they can provide an admirable base for a high-quality model.

Etched-brass kits are available from several sources including Sidelines, Blacksmith Models, CRT Kits, Hurn Models and David J Parkins. While some of these will be all-brass construction (with detail castings in white metal or brass), others will have resin parts

Westdale aluminium-bodied coach kit – old technology maybe, but capable of being built into some high-quality models. This is an LMS 57ft TPO vehicle under construction.

Westdale 'Midland Pullman' power car – another regular performer on 'Gifford Street', powered by twin ABC motor bogies and fitted with a DCC sound chip specially blown by South West Digital. The six-car set was built and painted by Richard Dockerill.

such as roof, seating and other details. A reasonable level of skill in soldering and etched-brass kit construction will be needed to build a model from one of these kits. Although passenger coaches might be considered comparatively easy items of rolling stock to build, depending on prototype they can be fairly complex and time-consuming models involving a lot of repetitive work. This is especially true in the case of non-compartment (suburban) stock or multiple units, which will have plenty of doors to contend with, each requiring a door handle, grab rail, door bumper and three hinges. Coaches with recessed doors or clerestory roofs can often present the modeller with the same level of complexity as a large locomotive kit.

For those who don't want to attempt etched-brass coach construction, a growing number of kits are now available in injection-moulded plastic or resin. With body components and other parts produced in these materials, door-hinge and other details are already incorporated in the bodysides, simplifying construction. Ian Kirk was one of the first exponents of 7mm-scale plastic coach kits, using a system of modular construction based around standardized door, window and other body components to produce a wide range of LNER, LMS, GWR and Southern coach types. Easy-Build is a more recent entrant to the O-gauge market, with its range of injection-moulded BR Mk1 coach and DMU kits. JLTRT also

Coaching stock is not just limited to carrying passengers. There are many other interesting vehicles available in kit form, such as the Newton Chambers double-deck car carrier built for the Eastern Region 'Anglo Scottish Car Carrier' service seen on the Westdale stand at Telford in 2014. Alongside is Wagon Lits stock for the London (Victoria)–Paris (Gare du Nord) 'Night Ferry' service.

Metro-Cammell DMU power car built from an aluminium-bodied Westdale kit. There are two Met-Cam units on 'Gifford Street', both the work of Norman Vickers.

More mixed media – this GWR Hawksworth coach kit from Hurn Models comprises pre-formed etched-brass sides, floor and other body and bogie components, resin roof and seats for first- and third-class compartments, plus a mixture of white-metal and lost-wax brass detail castings.

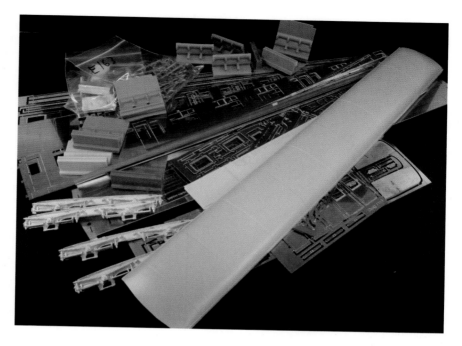

produces a growing range of coaching stock covering BR Mk1, Mk2 and some GWR and LNER types, all using resin sides, ends, roof and floor, with etched-brass and white-metal or lost-wax brass castings for bogies and detail items.

READY-TO-RUN

Many O-gauge modellers, myself included, will have at one time owned at least a few Lima BR Mk1 coaches. Despite being underscale and with only a Brake Second or Composite to choose from, these RTR models

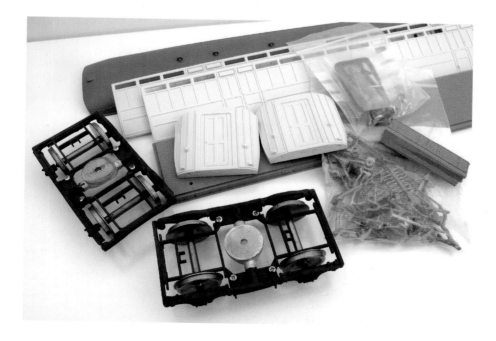

Cast-resin and lost-wax brass castings form the major parts of this JLTRT kit for a Gresley full brake. The bogies are easily assembled from bolt-together white-metal castings.

KIT-BUILD COACHING STOCK

Product	Supplier
BR Coaches (Including Multiple Units)	
Mk1 corridor	Easy-Build, JLTRT, Model Express, Modern Motive Power, Westdale
Mk1 non-corridor	Easy-Build, Westdale
Inspection Saloon	Easy-Build (WR), Westdale
TPO	JLTRT
Horsebox	CRT, JLTRT
Mk2	JLTRT, PR Model Railway Products, Westdale
HST/Mk3	PR Model Railway Products
Pullman	Westdale (Steel-aluminium clad, 'K' type and 1960 Met-Cam)
Diesel 'Midland Pullman'	Westdale
BR 'Heritage' DMUs	Easy-Build, Westdale
'Hastings'/'Tadpole'/ 'Thumper'	Peter Clark
Class 142/143/144 'Pacer'	PR Model Railway Products
'Sprinter'/'Super Sprinter'	Peter Clark
'Networker'/Class 325 EMUs	Peter Clark
2 HAP	CRT, Peter Clark
2 NOL/3 SUB	Roxey Mouldings
2 EPB/4 EPB/MLV/4	Peter Clark
CIG/4 VEP	
Post-Privatization	
'Networker Turbo'/ 'Turbostar' 'Voyager'/'Super Voyager'	Peter Clark
BR GUV/'Super' GUV	GH Plant, PR Model Railway Products
GWR/WR	
Collett bow-ended	JLTRT, Haywood Railway, Orion, Westdale
Flat ended and non-corridor	Westdale
Hawksworth	Haywood Railway, Hurn Models

Product	Supplier
Toplight, Dynamometer car J	LTRT
Auto trailers	JLTRT, Orion, Westdale
TPO	Westdale
Super Saloons, Centenary stock	Gladiator Models
Clerestory stock	CRT, Slater's
Four-wheel coaches	Roxey Mouldings, Slater's
Horsebox	Parkside
LMS/LMR	
Stanier Period II, 'Porthole'	Haywood Railway, Ian Kirk, Sidelines, Westdale
Period II	Westdale
Push/Pull	Sidelines, Westdale
LMS non-corridor	CRT, Ian Kirk, Westdale
1937 'Coronation Scot'	Sidelines, Westdale
District Engineers Saloon	Sidelines, Westdale
TPO	Westdale
Horsebox	CRT
MR Clayton	Gladiator Models, Sidelines
LNER/ER	
Gresley corridor	JLTRT, Ian Kirk
Gresley non-corridor	Ian Kirk
LNER articulated stock	Ian Kirk
LNER Tourist stock	Ian Kirk, Westdale
Thompson corridor	CRT, Sidelines
Thompson non-corridor	CRT
Horsebox	Parkside
SR/SR	
Maunsell corridor	CRT, Ian Kirk, Roxey Mouldings, Slater's, Westdale
Bulleid corridor	CRT, Westdale
'Devon Belle' observation car	Westdale
LSWR stock	Roxey Mouldings
CCT/PMV	CRT, Slater's

have provided the backbone of passenger services on many O-gauge layouts since the mid-1970s. Although no longer manufactured, second-hand examples regularly turn up for sale at reasonable prices, depending on condition. Several specialist businesses provide detailing and conversion or replacement parts and with a fair amount of work a scale-dimensioned model can result. With the further addition of pre-printed overlays a variety of convincing BR Mk1 types can be produced in early or late BR liveries as well as the later 'corporate' blue and grey. Firms such as Aquitrain produce RTR Lima conversions to a high standard for purchase to order or 'off the shelf', as well as selling pre-printed overlays matched to BR paint samples.

Ready-to-run Bachmann/Tower Brass BR Mk1 and GWR Collett coaches are also no longer available, although examples do appear for sale from time to time on eBay or advertised in the model press. Currently,

Heljan is the main producer of O-gauge RTR coaching stock with its range of BR Mk1 coaches, including a 57ft (17,374mm) Full Brake (BG) and General Utility Van (GUV), all available in various liveries. American manufacturer MTH (Mike's Train House) is the latest manufacturer to introduce a range of British-outline RTR coaches, with its models of Stanier 'Period III' stock, available for fine- or coarse-scale standards. The range includes Brake First (BFK), First Compartment (FK), Second Open (SO), and Full Brake (BG) in LMS maroon, LMS blue and silver 'Coronation Scot', BR 'blood and custard', BR maroon or BR blue (Full Brake only). Coaches are sold either singly, or as sets of two or three vehicles. Bogies are also available to purchase separately, along with three-rail conversion kits for coarse-scale layout owners.

Ready-to-run Great Western is represented by Lionheart Trains, which produces an auto-coach (also

Heljan RTR BR Mk1 coach – the appearance of these models is rather spoilt by their somewhat slab-sided appearance. However, this is not too noticeable if they only run in a rake without other makes of coaches to compare them with.

Lionheart Trains GWR auto-coach in weathered 1950s BR livery.

available with onboard DCC sound effects), with a two-coach 'B set' and four-coach Birmingham non-corridor set promised for later in 2016. Currently no manufacturer offers RTR, SR or more modern coaches, although specialist firms like Golden Age do produce a limited range of high-quality models of various coach types including LNER and SR types, GWR 'Centenary' stock, 'Super Saloons' and Pullmans. Batches of these hand-built models are built to order, but customers can expect to pay between £500–£800 per coach, depending on type and livery required.

MOTIVE POWER

READY-TO-RUN FOR ALL POCKETS

Apart from producing a few resin-cast buildings, mainstream UK manufacturers Bachmann and Hornby have both abandoned O gauge, allowing Danish manufacturer Heljan to dominate the UK market with its new generation of RTR locomotives. Since 2005, Heljan has consistently worked its way through most of the British diesel fleet, including iconic types such as the 'Hymek', 'Warship', 'Western', 'Deltic', *Falcon* and Type 4 1Co-Co-1 (Class 40), as well as the less glamourous Class 20, 26, 31, 37 and workhorse Class 47. The Heljan range has been a great boost to modellers of early diesels in the BR period and the introduction of the Class 60 now means that there is a relatively modern-period diesel also available in RTR form.

All have detailed injection-moulded plastic bodies with heavy diecast chassis, powerful twin-motor bogies and working lights. Some are also fitted with working fans and all are easily converted to DCC operation by removing the body, as you would with a smaller-scale loco, removing the 12V DC circuit board and replacing it with a DCC decoder. Heljan's first steam outline release, a GWR 61xx 'Large Prairie' is scheduled for 2017, with a 43xx 'Mogul' and A3/A4 in the pipeline. Also due for release in 2016 is an RTR model of the British Thomson Houston Class 15 diesel from the Little Loco Company, a new name in the O-gauge arena. Produced with the cooperation of the Class 15 Preservation Society, this promises to be an interesting addition to the range of RTR early diesel types now available to O-gauge modellers.

Since 2009, Lionheart Trains has concentrated on low-volume models of GWR prototypes of extremely high quality. Starting with the 64xx/74xx pannier tank, and 'Small Prairie' tanks, followed by a 43xx 'Mogul', available as 12V DC or DCC sound versions, with a BR Standard 3MT 2-6-2T to come in 2017. Dapol has also entered the O-gauge RTR arena with its realistically priced 'Terrier' 0-6-0T, available in a number of different liveries, followed by the long-lived Class 08 diesel shunter. The 'Terrier' has already proved to be a popular choice for modellers and their 57xx Pannier should also be received with equal enthusiasm.

Ready-to-run O-gauge locos can also be kit-bashed – the Heljan Class 47 formed the basis for 57 001 'Freightliner Pioneer', as modified by Edward Bird and seen on a visit to 'Gifford Street'.

The GWR 'Small Prairie' tank was the second locomotive to be released by Lionheart Trains. Like the earlier 64xx model, it was available in analogue and DCC sound versions.

All are available as DCC ready or DCC/DCC sound versions.

Currently no manufacturers produce RTR BR, LMS, LNER or SR locomotives, although a limited amount of San Cheng all-brass models remain available from Finescale Brass and Tower Models. Specialist firms like Golden Age, Laurie Loveless and Sette Models produce limited numbers of high-quality hand-assembled models. DJH also produces limited numbers of ready-built and built to order locomotives from its extensive range of kits. Consequently, prices of all these items are considerably more than the mass-produced RTR items, but will reflect level of detail, locomotive type and livery required.

All of the RTR locomotives mentioned so far have been main-line types, but there is also a growing range of industrial locomotive types, which are ideal for smaller layouts. The Ixion Models Hudswell Clarke 0-6-0ST has been around since 2012 and has also proved a popular choice of prototype. Produced for 12V DC operation out of the box, DCC sound-installed versions are also available from many retailers, although fitting DCC is a simple job by removing the top of the body moulding to access the decoder socket, removing the blanking plate and installing a decoder. Ixion's second model is a small Fowler 0-4-0 diesel shunter, ideal for small industrial layouts.

Following Ixion's decision to drop out of the UK market, Chris Klein formed a partnership with Chris Baston of Dragon Models to produce a Peckett 'E' Class 0-4-0ST under the Minerva Models label. Following the success of this model, their next pro-

1st Livery Sample
Copyright 2016 Dapol Ltd

Despite its lengthy delay, the Dapol Class 08 is still one of the most eagerly anticipated O-gauge RTR models and should prove immensely popular with both steam-age and diesel-era modellers.

ject will see the introduction of a larger industrial locomotive – the Kerr Stuart 'Victory' Class 0-6-0T. Although only ten were built in 1917 for the Inland Waterways & Docks Department, three ended up in GWR service, two surviving into BR days, with the last being scrapped in 1955. For those wanting a larger industrial type, this should prove ideal.

*The Ixion Fowler 0-4-0 diesel shunter – this example formed the subject of a heavy rebuild for a project by **British Railway Modelling's** Howard Smith and is another ideal candidate for a small shunting-type layout, or for use in a lineside industry.*

KIT-BUILDING ADDS VARIETY

Whilst RTR models can save valuable modelling time, the range of available locomotive types is still quite limited, especially for the modeller of steam outline locos. Kit building will add much needed variety to the O-gauge locomotive fleet. Most kits now have components like boiler, smokebox, tenders and diesel loco bodies, supplied ready formed instead of 'flat packed' so that there is no need for the purchaser to roll sheet metal. Other kits may have a resin-cast boiler, smokebox and firebox assemblies included, or available as direct replacements (as in some JLTRT kits, for example), which can simplify construction considerably.

Etched parts will have rivet detail and fold lines half-etched and all rivets will need to be punched before the various parts are cut off the fret for assembly. Fold lines will also need to be scored to give a sharp, clean fold and checked with a square for absolute accuracy during assembly. Once etched parts have been cut off the fret they will need any cusps and high spots removing with a file. Parts will also need to be thoroughly clean before being soldered in position, using a fibreglass brush to burnish both surfaces. The workpiece also will need to be cleaned after working sessions to remove any build-up of excess flux. For those not familiar with soldering or not used to etched brass construction, a most useful beginner's guide has been produced by Jim McGeown in the form of a series of frequently asked questions, comprehensively illustrated. *O-Gauge Etched Kit Building* is available from Connoisseur Models and is recommended reading for modellers in all scales contemplating etched kit construction.

JLTRT 3F 0-6-0 under construction – much of the hard work has been taken out of the build, with the use of a resin-cast firebox/boiler/smokebox assembly and resin tender tank. This kit is being altered to represent a specific locomotive, with later detail differences including Stanier-pattern brake standard and extended tender side sheets.

Another JLTRT kit on the workbench – as with all JLTRT diesel kits, the Class 17 'Clayton' is mainly high-grade cast-resin construction, making assembly a fairly easy affair using suitable cyanoacrylate adhesives (superglue).

Flying Scotsman in 1969 condition with its second tender (from A4 60009) prior to its ill-fated USA tour. Like all DJH products, this limited-edition kit is built from a mixture of pewter boiler, smokebox and running plate, etched-brass cab and tender, with white-metal and lost-wax brass detail castings.

Stanier 5MT 2-6-0 built from a David Andrews etched-brass kit. Powered by a Portascap motor and gearbox, No.42968 has been one of the regular performers on 'Gifford Street' over the years.

Crosti kit-bash – some extreme surgery and a heavily modified Seven Models kit was used by Tony Geary as the basis for this Crosti 9F in original condition. Built for Andrew Baldwin, Wellingborough (15A) based No.92026 is seen on a running in turn at 'Gifford Street'.

The dying art of scratch-building – Geoff Holt's superb LMS 'Royal Scot' Class 4-6-0 No.6170 British Legion makes a guest appearance in the early days of 'Gifford Street'. Built for David Jenkinson more than two decades ago, the prototype was a rebuild of the high-pressure experimental locomotive, Fury.
TONY WRIGHT/COURTESY BRITISH RAILWAY MODELLING

KIT-BUILT LOCOMOTIVES

Locomotive Kits

BR Steam	DJH, Modern Outline Kits, Scorpio Models
BR Diesel	DJH, JLTRT, Judith Edge Kits, Modern Motive Power, PR Model Railway Products, Steve Beattie, Tower Collection
GWR and constituents	JLTRT, Mercian, Scorpio Models, Slater's, Springside,
LMS and constituents	DJH, JLTRT, Laurie Griffin, Modern Outline Kits, Tower Collection
LNER and constituents	Ace Products, DJH
SR and constituents	Ace Products, Modern Outline Kits

Locomotives

BRITISH RAILWAYS

Description	Manufacturer	DC/DCC
'Britannia' 7MT 4-6-2	55H Models	DCC sound
Duke of Gloucester 8P 4-6-2	55H Models	DCC sound
9F 2-10-0	55H Models or Golden Age	DCC sound
DP1 Prototype *Deltic*	L.H. Loveless	DC (option for DCC sound)
Class 05 0-6-0 Hunslet diesel shunter	Heljan	DC
Class 08 0-6-0 350hp diesel electric	Dapol	DC/DCC sound
Class 15 BTH Bo-Bo	Little Loco Company	DCC sound ready
Class 25/1 Bo-Bo diesel electric	Heljan	DC
Class 31 A1A-A1A diesel electric	Heljan	DC
Class 42 'Warship' B-B diesel hydraulic	Heljan	DC
Class 45 1Co-Co1 diesel electric	Heljan	DC
Class 55 'Deltic' diesel electric	L.H. Loveless	DC (option for DCC sound)
Class 60 Co-Co diesel electric	Heljan	DC
Brush prototype diesel electric *Falcon*	Heljan	DC
AC Cars four-wheel railbus	Heljan	DC

GREAT WESTERN RAILWAY/BR (WR)

1361 0-6-0ST	Tower Brass or Heljan	DC (option for DCC/DCC sound)
14xx 0-4-2T	Tower Brass	DC (option for DCC/DCC sound)
45xx 2-6-2T	Lionheart	DC/DCC sound
43xx 'Mogul' 2-6-0	Lionheart or Heljan	DC/DCC sound
'City' 4-4-0	San Cheng	DC
GWR/BR 'Star' 4-6-0	Golden Age	DCC sound
61xx 2-6-2T	Heljan	DC
64xx 0-6-0PT	Lionheart	DC/DCC sound
57xx 8750 0-6-0PT	Tower Brass/Dapol/Minerva	DC/DCC sound
'Castle' 4-6-0	Golden Age	DCC sound
60xx 'King' 4-6-0	Tower Brass or Golden Age	DC (option for DCC/DCC sound)
68xx 'Grange' 4-6-0	San Cheng	DC
78xx 'Manor' 4-6-0	San Cheng	DC
'Razor edge' railcar (Nos19–33)	Tower Brass	DC (option for DCC/DCC sound)
'Razor edge' Parcels railcar (No.34)	Tower Brass	DC (option for DCC/DCC sound)

LONDON MIDLAND & SCOTTISH RAILWAY/BR (LMR) AND CONSTITUENT COMPANIES

L&Y 'Pug' 0-4-0ST	Tower Brass	DC (option for DCC/DCC sound)
'Patriot' 4-6-0	Tower Brass	DC (option for DCC/DCC sound)
'Jubilee' 4-6-0	San Cheng	DC
'Princess Royal' 4-6-2	Golden Age or L.H. Loveless	DCC sound
Streamlined 'Coronation' 4-6-2	Golden Age	DCC sound
'Duchess' 4-6-2	L.H. Loveless	DCC sound

continued overleaf

LONDON NORTH EASTERN RAILWAY/BR (ER) AND CONSTITUENT COMPANIES

Replica A1 4-6-2 *Tornado*	Golden Age	DCC sound
A1 4-6-2	L H Loveless or Golden Age	DCC sound
A2 4-6-2	Golden Age	DCC sound
A3 4-6-2	Golden Age/L.H. Loveless/Heljan	DCC sound
A4 4-6-2	Golden Age/L.H. Loveless/Heljan	DCC sound
B1 4-6-0	San Cheng	DC
J39 0-6-0	Tower Brass	DC (option for DCC/DCC sound)
J50 0-6-0T	San Cheng	DC
P2 2-8-2	Golden Age or L.H. Loveless	DCC sound
V2 2-6-2	San Cheng	DC

SOUTHERN RAILWAY/BR (SR) AND CONSTITUENT COMPANIES

A1/A1X 'Terrier' 0-6-0T	Dapol or Finescale Brass	DC or DCC sound
'Schools' 4-4-0	San Cheng	DC
'WC'/'BoB' 4-6-2	Golden Age	DCC sound
Rebuilt 'Merchant Navy' 4-6-2	Golden Age	DCC sound

INDUSTRIAL

Fowler 0-4-0 diesel mechanical	Ixion	DC (option for DCC/DCC sound)
Hudswell-Clarke 0-6-0ST	Ixion	DC (option for DCC/DCC sound)
Peckett 'E' Class 0-4-0ST	Minerva Models	DCC ready
Kerr Stuart 'Victory' Class 0-6-0T	Minerva Models	DCC ready

UK Outline Rolling Stock

Description	Manufacturer	Availability
GWR/BR Auto coach	Lionheart	GWR/BR liveries – also available with DCC sound
GWR/BR 'B-Set'		
GWR/BR Birmingham set		
GWR/BR Collett Corridor		
Brake Third	Tower Brass	
BR Mk1 coaches/GUV	Heljan	various types/liveries available
BR 16T mineral wagon	Lionheart	various types/liveries
RCH 1927 end door/coke wagons	Lionheart	various liveries including private owner
14T tank wagon	Lionheart	various liveries for Class A and Class B products
Class B tank wagon	Heljan	various liveries for Class B products
'Catfish'/'Dogfish' ballast hopper	Heljan	
VAA van/OAA wagon	Heljan	
Cargowaggon IWB/IPE/IGE	Heljan	Cargowaggon, Corus, various liveries

62C Models
North British Railway loco kits
www.62cmodels.com
email: petermullen@btinternet.com

ABS
Loco and rolling-stock kits and components, mostly white metal
Tel: 01202 672891

Ace Locomotive Kits
Etched-brass loco kits
www.a4ace@supanet.com
email: a4ace@supanet.com

Ace Trains
'Brilliantly old-fashioned' standard-scale O gauge
Tel: 0207 727 1592
www.acetrainslondon.com
email: info@ace-trains.co.uk

Alba Railway Models
Caledonian Railway kits
www.albarailwaymodels.co.uk
email: enquiries@albarailwaymodels.co.uk

David Andrews
Etched-brass steam outline locomotive kits
Tel: 01242 672744
www.locomotivekits.com
email: davidandrews@locomotivekits.com

Aquitrain
Lima coach conversions, locos, wagons and spares, coach overlays
Tel: 0035 553 632 311
www.aquitrain.com
email: maurice@aquitrain.com

Blacksmith Models
Etched-brass coach kits
Tel: 01652 680243
www.blacksmithmodels.com
email: blacksmithmodels@aol.com

Buzz Models
Modern image wagon kits, cast figures, brick papers, turned brass items
Tel: 01923 672809
www.buzzmodels.co.uk
email: buzzmodels@gmail.com

Eddie Bye
GWR coach headboards
Tel: 01526 344426 (until 8.00pm)
email: eddie.bye@virgin.net

Peter Clark Models
Diesel and electric multiple-unit and rolling-stock kits, parts and accessories
Tel: 020 8464 0696
www.peterclarkkits.com
email: enquiries@peterclarkkits.com

Connoisseur Models
Etched-brass loco and rolling stock kits
Tel: 01544 318263
www.jimmcgeown.com

Peter Cowling
Coach interior components and roof sections
Tel: 0116 2350237

CRT Kits
Etched-brass coach and van kits
Tel: 01279 876402
www.crtkits.gbr.cc
email: info@crtkits.gbr.cc

Mike Danby
Loco builder, commissions and 'kit rescue' service
Tel: 0113 287 3997
email: mikedanby3379@aol.com

Dapol
RTR locos and rolling stock (DCC sound available)
Tel: 01691 774455
www.dapol.co.uk

continued overleaf

SUPPLIERS *continued*

DJH Engineering Ltd
Cast white-metal loco kits and factory built ready-to-run
Tel: 01207 500050
www.djhmodelloco.co.uk
email: sales@djhmodelloco.co.uk

DJ Modelmaking Services
Kit and scratch building service
Tel: 07963 591065
www.djamodels.moonfruit.com
email: dja.info@blueyonder.co.uk

Dragon Models
Loco and rolling stock kits
Tel: 02920 531246
www.dragonmodelswales.co.uk
email: chrisbasten@fsmail.net

D&S Models
Etched-brass rolling-stock kits
Tel: 01763 288353

Easy-Build 1st Class Coaches
DMU and coach kits
Tel: 01840 213295 (until 9.00pm)
www.easybuildcoaches.co.uk
email: shawn_ easybuild@btinternet.com

Judith Edge Kits
Etched-brass loco kits
Tel: 01226 722309
www.ukmodelshops.co.uk/catalogues/judithedge.html
email: edgemd@aol.com

EDM Models
Narrow-gauge loco kits
Tel: 01904 331973
www.ngtrains.com
email: paul@ngtrains.com

Electrifying Trains
Ready-built Electric Multiple Units
Tel: 0208 440 5918
www.electrifyingtrains.co.uk
email: info@electrifyingtrains.co.uk

Finescale Brass
RTR brass-built locomotives (DCC sound available)
Tel: 01132 794872
www.finescalebrass.co.uk
email: john@finescalebrass.co.uk

Colin Flannery
Scale model constructor
Tel: 01775 750505

Furness Railway Wagon Co.
Tel: 01229 468206
www.ukmodelshops.co.uk/catalogue/furness
email: furnessrailway@hotmail.com

Dan Garrett
SER/SECR/SR loco and rolling-stock kits
www.serkits.com
email: serkits1@aol.com

Alan Gibson Workshop
Etched-brass loco and rolling-stock kits
Tel: 0161 678 1607
www.alangibsonworkshop.co.uk
email: sales@alangibsonworkshop.co.uk

Gladiator Kits
Etched-brass loco and rolling-stock kits
Tel: 01455 291236
www.gladiatormodelkits.co.uk

Golden Age Models
RTR brass-built locomotives (DCC sound available)
Tel: 01929 480210
www.goldenagemodels.net

Gosling
Etched-brass overlays for Bulleid WC/BoB or MN wheels
Tel: 01363 84075

Laurie Griffin Miniatures
Loco and rolling stock kits, Shedmaster Models, loco detail castings
www.lgminiatures.co.uk
email: info@lgminiatures.co.uk

Haywood Railway
Rolling stock kits and components
Tel: 01889 881610
email: gp.gill@yahoo.co.uk

Heljan
RTR locos and rolling stock
www.heljan.dk
email: heljanuk@yahoo.co.uk

Hobby Holidays
Rolling-stock kits, components, and practical modelling courses
Tel: 01427 848979
www.hobbyholidays.co.uk
email: phil@hobbyholidays.co.uk

Hobbyhorse Developments
Lost-wax brass-cast locomotive parts
Tel: 0208 3024913
www.hobbyhorse.co.uk
email: info@hobbyhorse.co.uk

Howes Models Ltd
Heljan importer and distributor, RailMatch paints
Tel: 01865 848000

J & M Hughes
Coach-building service, EMU/Pullman detail castings
Tel: 01903 784011
email: mikehughes74@hotmail.co.uk

Hurn Models
Rolling stock kits
Tel: 01202 475164
email: hurnmodels@thehilliers.plus.com

Invertrain
MTH coaches, Wayoh coach bogies
email: enquiries@invertrain.com
www.invertrain.com

Isinglass
LNER loco and carriage drawings
Tel: 07973 768080 (evenings)
www.Isinglass-Models.co.uk

Ixion Model Railways Ltd.
RTR locomotives
www.ixionmodels.com
email: info@ixionmodels.com

Brian Jones
Radio control and digital sound
Tel: 01790 752042
www.brianjones.free-online.co.uk
email: bjones@paston.co.uk

JPL Models
White-metal and brass loco and rolling stock fittings
Tel: 01942 896138
email: jplmodels@yahoo.co.uk

Just Like The Real Thing
Multi-media loco and rolling stock kits
Tel: 01924 222988
www.justliketherealthing.co.uk
email: laurie@justliketherealthing.co.uk

KB Scale
7mm narrow-gauge kits
Tel: 01883 335846
www.kbscale.com
email: news@kbscale.com

Kemilway
Hand-built locos and coaches
Tel: 01449 781010
www.kemilway.com
email: peter.dawson2@btconnect.com

Ken's Profiles
Etched-brass kits of Metropolitan Railway locos and stock, profile milling service
Tel: 01945 870060
email: ken.degroome@btinternet.com

Alan Kettlewell
Kit-building service
Tel: 01748 834339
email: alankettlewell@sky.com

continued overleaf

Ian Kirk
Coach-building kits and components
Tel: 01592 620105
www.iankirkmodels.co.uk
email: iankirkmodels@hotmail.co.uk

Kristunas Models
Modelmaker
Tel: 01608 662313
www.kristunasmodels.com
email: kristunas@btinternet.com

Lanky Kits
Loco and rolling-stock kits of LYR prototypes
Tel: 01772 493309
www.lankykits.co.uk
email: info@lankykits.co.uk

Lionheart Trains
RTR locomotives and rolling stock (DCC sound available)
Tel: 01453 833302
email: sales@lionhearttrains.com
www.lionhearttrains.com

Little Loco Company
Loco kits, RTR Class 15
www.littleloco.co.uk

Lochgorm Kits
Highland Railway loco, rolling-stock and other kits
Tel: 01373 455194
www.lochgormkits.co.uk
email: lochgormkits@copps.freeuk.com

L.H. Loveless & Co.
RTR brass-built locomotives (DCC sound available)
Tel: 01423 712446
www.loveless.co.uk
email: lawrie@loveless.co.uk

Magnificent Carriages
Batch-built RTR trains from the post-Group companies
Tel: 07531 925100
www.magnificentcarriages.co.uk
email: info@magnificentcarriages.co.uk

Masterpiece Models
Ready-to-run locos
Tel: 01202 700050
www.masterpiecemodels.co.uk
email: masterpiecemodels@trceurope.f9.co.uk

Meteor Models
Etched-brass loco and rolling-stock kits
Tel: 01604 671731
www.meteormodels.com
email: tim_hughes@ntlworld.com

Minerva Model Railways
Tel: 02920 531246
www.minervamodelrailways.co.uk
email: sales@minervamodelrailways.co.uk

M&M Models
EMKDE etched-brass rolling-stock kits
Tel: 01202 386195
email: onthewagon22@hotmail.co.uk

Model Express
Etched-brass BR Mk1 coach kits
Tel: 01423 860505
email: daveclarke25@hotmail.co.uk

Modern Outline Kits
Etched-brass steam outline loco kits
Tel: 01522 531861
www.modernoutline.co.uk
email: sales@modernoutline.co.uk

MSC Models
Motors and gearboxes
Tel: 020 8398 2415

Northants Model Railway Supplies
Loco and rolling-stock kits, parts
Tel: 01604 768843
www.nmrs-models.co.uk
email: nmrs-models@btinternet.com

Orion Rail Kits
Collett and Hawksworth coach kits
Tel: 01892 537236
email: j.d.colebrooke@talk21.com

Parkside Dundas
Plastic injection-moulded rolling-stock kits
Tel: 01592 640896
www.parksidedundas.co.uk
email: sales@parksidedundas.co.uk

Parliamentary Trains
Early railway rolling stock kits
Tel: 07771 508085
www.parlytrains.co.uk
email: steve@parlytrains.co.uk

Peartree Engineering
O-gauge model railway parts
Tel: 01379 60800
www.modelrailwayparts.com
email: info@modelrailwayparts.com

Port Wynnstay Models
Standard- and narrow-gauge kits, tram parts, architectural components
www.portwynnstay.co.uk
email: phil@portwynnstay.co.uk

Powsides
Pre-printed wagon sides, kits, transfers
Tel: 01279 876402
www.powsides.co.uk
email: sales@powsides.co.uk

Premier Components
Chassis and valve gear components
Tel: 01606 554616
www.premiercomponents.co.uk
email: bill@premiercomponents.co.uk

PR Model Railway Products
Class 144 and 142/3 DMU kits, flush glazing kits
Tel: 07807 225801
email: prmp@fsmail.net

Quainton Road Models
Great Central Railway and Metropolitan Railway locos and stock
Tel: 01566 880157
www.quainton-road-models.co.uk
email: contact@quainton-road-models.co.uk

Radley Models
London Underground loco, rolling-stock and vehicle kits
Tel: 01425 479377
www.radleymodels.co.uk

Ragstone Models
Loco and rolling-stock kits, details and accessories
email: andy@ragstonemodels.co.uk

Redcraft Ltd
Loco kits built to order
Tel: 02920 251049
email: redcraft@ntlbusiness.com

Roxey Mouldings
Loco and coach kits, steel wheels, motors and gearboxes
Tel: 01932 245439
www.roxeymouldings.co.uk

Mike Russell Models
Kit-building service
Tel: 01872 272325
email: michael.russell11@btopenworld.com

Scorpio Models
Etched-brass GWR loco and rolling-stock kits
Tel: 01633 279897
email: scorpiomodels@hotmail.co.uk

Sette Models
Museum-quality model locos
Tel: 0131 667 3405
www.settemodels.co.uk
email: settemodels@gmail.com

continued overleaf

Seven Models
Etched-brass loco kits
Tel: 01633 892242
email: sevenmodels@live.co.uk

Warren Shephard
GWR/WR loco kits and components
Tel: 01766 770739
www.warrenshephard.com
email: warren_shephard@btinternet.com

Sidelines
Coach kits and components, ready-built coaches
Tel: 01228 521671
www.sidelinescoaches.co.uk
email: malcolm.binns@sky.com

Signature Railway Kits
Loco and rolling stock kits
Tel: 01282 458987
email: john1067@hotmail.co.uk

Slater's Plastikard
Locomotive and rolling stock kits, motor/gearboxes
Tel: 01629 734053
www.slatersplastikard.com

SM Models
Loco and rolling-stock kits
Tel: 01773 782848

Springside Models
Cast white-metal loco kits and detail parts
Tel: 01803 813749
www.springsidemodels.com
email: springsidemodels@btinternet.com

Team Track Trading
Specialist in German and American railways
Tel: 01209 213554
www.teamtracktrading.co.uk
email: accounts@teamtracktrading.co.uk

TMS Models
Commission built locos and rolling stock
Tel: 01625 829805
www.tmsmodels.biz
email: terrysmith@tmsmodels.biz

Walsworth Models
Loco and rolling stock kits
Tel: 01952 510198
www.walsworthmodels.co.uk
email: walsworth.models@virgin.net

WEP Models
Etched-brass GWR wagon and van kits
Tel: 0121 429 4086

Westdale Coaches
Coach and DMU kits
Tel: 01628 482493

Cliff Williams
DCC/DCC sound-fitting service, Heljan stockist
Tel: 01592 642422
www.cliffwilliams.co.uk/models

CHAPTER EIGHT

GETTING THAT LINESIDE LOOK

There is a world of difference between a model railway and a model of a railway. One can end up looking like a glorified train set, while the other may have that indefinable something we like to call 'atmosphere'. I think it was David Jenkinson who suggested that the test of a good layout was to see if it could still evoke the atmosphere of the real railway even when totally devoid of stock and locomotives. However, to get that authentic lineside look you do not have to be an expert on railway matters; it really comes down to a matter of observation. At art college, we were taught to draw what we see — not what we *think* we see — and the same principle applies to modelling. Observe the prototype, or if you can't do that, look at photographs in books, magazines, online, or on DVDs. But whatever you do, please don't model what you see on someone else's layout — more than likely they got it from someone else, who got it from someone who got it wrong in the first place.

For modellers of the BR period from the 1950s onwards, a good idea is to find some contemporary magazines of the period (such as the *Railway*

Not a train in sight — the view from behind Calvert Street signal box as RDD 590 — Dad's trusty old Ford Popular — waits at the level crossing. Careful use of contemporary road signs, advertisements and road vehicles adds period atmosphere on 'Gifford Street'. TONY WRIGHT/COURTESY BRITISH RAILWAY MODELLING

Magazine or *Trains Illustrated*), then take a look at some of the many colour albums now available. You may be surprised to see how many of those 'soot and whitewash' photographs in those old magazines were taken on colour stock. Half a century or so later, modern reprographics and print technology make them look as if they were taken yesterday. Reading contemporary accounts accompanied by colour photographs may give you a fresh new insight into the final years of the British steam age – and early diesel – railways.

AVOIDING THE OBVIOUS

Small layouts can give owners the opportunity to include a higher level of detail than larger layouts and these days there are plenty of castings, kits, figures and other accessories available. However, if you really want to make your layout more realistic, then do not overdo it and try to avoid the twee or the obvious clichés that appear on layout after layout. For example, the wedding party at the church porch and the burial party in the graveyard; the police chase or fire engine with blue flashing lights; the all-action fairground; the marching Guard's band; scantily clad ladies in bedroom windows and so on. Without wishing to spoil anyone's fun, these are all things that can instantly destroy any illusion of reality and make that difference between a model railway and a model of a railway. To make your layout more realistic, we are looking for the suspension of disbelief.

Figures in action poses are also best avoided – figures frozen in mid-stride or other actions can look unnatural and only emphasize the lack of movement. Movement can be suggested in other more subtle ways, for example by having the odd door open on buildings, a bicycle propped up against a wall, or arranging natural-looking groups – perhaps two people stopped to have a chat, reading a newspaper on a street corner, or leaning on a shovel in the coal yard. When painting miniature figures, make sure that you do not use gloss paint and also avoid using overly bright colours. Instead, try to keep to a fairly restrained use of colour and undercoat, first in white to highlight colours, or black to emphasize shadows. Use only matt colours to paint figures and other scenic details, varnishing where you need a satin finish. Again, look at the real thing – do not assume that tree trunks or telegraph poles are a uniform brown colour, or that roads are black, for example.

A group of track workers stand well clear of the running lines after replacing a check rail on 'Gifford Street'.

KIT-BASHING FOR PLEASURE

Although you may be content to run your layout with RTR locos and stock straight out of the box, building kits can add variety to your rolling stock. However, plastic rolling-stock kits can also provide an ideal starting point for kit-bashing, that is, turning the kit into a different type of vehicle from that which the kit manufacturer intended. For example, Parkside's GWR 'Toad' can also be converted to an earlier version with different suspension and buf-fers, or with a lot more involved work into a rebuilt Mess & Tool van. The Slater's GWR cattle van has the potential to be modified to make a later version of the same vehicle, or altered to create the BR 8 ton cattle van, a type not otherwise available in either kit or RTR form in 7mm. Other examples of kit-bashed O-gauge rolling stock are illustrated below. They may inspire you to have a go — there are plenty of reference books on 'Big Four' and BR rolling stock, or look at Paul Bartlett's excellent website to whet the appetite.

Plastic kits are ideal for a spot of kit-bashing. This Parkside GWR Diagram AA19 'Toad' Brake Van has several simple additions — extra 'A'-framing on the bodysides, sandpipes added below the verandah end, safety straps to the brake gear, and the BR low-level style of vacuum pipes, as it represents a 'piped' vehicle with through pipe and brake-setting valve (also modelled on the verandah interior).

The same kit during the process of conversion to the earlier Diagram AA15 'Toad' with replacement 'J'-hanger suspension, GWR self-contained buffers and GWR-style Instanter couplings. The central strut at the verandah end supports the fragile curved top member and will be removed once the roof is permanently fixed in place.

A much more involved rebuild into a Departmental Mess and Tool Van. Vehicles like these were attached to cranes and ballast cleaners to provide messing facilities for the crews, several being converted in GWR days, others in the BR period. Some of the work involved includes verandah ends planked in, larger central windows at each end, new side windows, additional 'A' framing, lamp irons and grab rails, new vacuum brake cylinder, pushrods, brake lever and guide, 'J'-hanger suspension and GWR self-contained buffers.

Slater's GWR Cattle Wagon (left) provides the basis for conversion to the BR 8 ton cattle wagon. Alterations include revised higher ends with new diagonal strapping in place of the older 'X' bracing, revised top doors with access hole for staff working inside the vehicle, BR axle guards and axle boxes, and Morton-style brakes.

A completed BR cattle wagon – the new roof is rolled from a piece of brass sheet, easily cut to size with a 'Skrawker' cutting tool. Just score, bend and snap – it really is that easy. Bauxite livery is a cheat using Halford's Red Oxide acrylic car primer. When weathered down it looks just like – weathered bauxite!

The Parkside Gunpowder Van is another candidate for conversion – BR equipped many of these 9ft (2.7m) wheelbase vehicles with the automatic vacuum brake. Alterations to the kit include new Oleo buffers, vacuum cylinder and low-level vac pipes, brake lever (all ABS white metal) and nickel-silver tie bar between the axle guards.

The finished vacuum-braked Gunpowder Van makes a slightly different model to a straight kit build. A fret of lost-wax brass detail castings from the spares box furnished a pair of padlocks for the doors, though unfortunately I have no idea of their origin.

Another Parkside conversion – BR converted a number of Grampus ballast wagons into winch and roller wagons for Rail Loader Sets. Marshalled at either end of a number of 'Salmon' rail-carrying wagons, they were used for lifting and carrying long lengths of continuous welded rail before the introduction of modern fully mechanized handling equipment.

White-metal and etched kits can also make suitable kit-bashing projects. This GWR Diagram M14 'Loriot M' (one of Jim McGeown's 'Skill-builder' kits from his Connoisseur Models range) has been altered to a through-piped BR-built 'Lowmac WE' – the Drott excavator is a delightful white-metal kit from Langley Models, with added detail.

WHATEVER THE WEATHER

Just about everything on 'Gifford Street' is weathered. From road vehicles and buildings to locomotives, a degree of weathering can add character and a sense of mass, although there is no need to overdo it. Wherever possible, try to work from a photograph of the vehicle you are modelling, but don't slavishly follow it. There is no need to use proprietary weathering colours: Humbrol matt black (33), matt Khaki (26 or 29) and matt white (34) form my basic weathering kit. Stage painters have used a similar restrained palette for theatrical back scenes for years, so we can't go far wrong! I prefer Humbrol enamels, but you may have your own favourite brand, or prefer acrylics, in which case you will have to modify the methods described here. I also prefer to brush paint, so as to give more variation between models. Find something on which to mix colours – old tin lids, CD cases and the like – paint stirrers (cocktail sticks or coffee stirrers), plenty of white spirit and a jar to pour the paint into, plus a selection of brushes. Weathering takes its toll on brushes, which will become quite worn very quickly, especially if you indulge in a lot of dry brushing. Keep them separate from your 'best' brushes and do not store brushes upright in a jar. It might look more arty, but this is the best way to end up with brushes that look like mops and are full of dust, so store them in a box or drawer, or both.

Most rolling stock can be split into three basic areas for weathering: underframe; bodysides and ends; and interior (or roof in the case of vans). Using our three basic matt colours, we can achieve a variety of effects merely by altering the amount of black, white or Khaki in the mix. Do not worry if you can't get exactly the same mix of paint, as no two wagons ever weathered to the same degree on the full-size railway. Underframes will receive much the same treatment regardless of whether they are steel or wood. Never use pure black; always make sure that it is 'knocked back' slightly by the addition of another colour. Mixing a little Khaki should give you the desired effect. Wheels and some parts of the underframe can appear quite dusty, so introduce a little more Khaki. Do not forget to paint buffers, axles and the backs of wheel sets, but keep paint away from bearings and wheel treads. Final highlighting of detail

Weathered wagons on 'Gifford Street'. These Lionheart 1927 RCH seven-plank opens are part of a large weathering job awaiting delivery to a client.

Weathering starts with a pristine wagon out of the box.

*The end result –
a Lionheart seven-plank
open-weathered using the
method described in
the text.*

can be achieved by gentle dry brushing with Khaki when dry.

Use a fairly dark matt black and matt Khaki mix diluted with white spirit for generally weathering stock. Flood the colour on the van or wagon body, then take a brush dipped in white spirit, wipe on a lint-free cloth or tissue and use the brush to lift off colour – applying colour, then washing it off little by little until the desired effect is achieved. Enamel paints have a longer drying time than acrylics, giving a little more time to 'work' the paint. Create streaking caused by water running down the bodyside by gentle downward strokes of the brush. Before the paint hardens, use a wide (1in/25mm or so) brush to give a more general streaking effect. Streaking and splashes caused by track dirt can be achieved by brushing upwards from the solebar, or by dry brushing when the main weathering has dried and hardened.

The paint should naturally flow into planking and gather in corners, along stanchions, diagonal strapping and so on, so when lifting paint be careful not to remove it from these areas. After flooding colour on to the vehicle, use a sponge or pad of tissue (avoid patterned kitchen towel) to lift excess paint. You can also flood white spirit on to force pigment into the edges of the strapping and so on. Employ the same method on steel-bodied vehicles, but use a sponge or wad of tissue to wipe paint down the bodyside – this will leave an uneven area of paint around the strapping and also drag some of the paint to give an irregular

streak effect. For really lazy modellers, there are even transfers for rust streaks available these days.

WAGON INTERIORS

Wagon interiors reflect the nature of the loads carried. For mineral wagons use the black/Khaki mix to suggest coal traffic or general use, or ring the changes with Dark Red Oxide (Humbrol 113 or Revell 37), adding a little black to vary the colour. This is more suitable for wagons carrying iron ore, scrap loads and so on, whereas mineral wagons used for chalk traffic will have a stark white interior. There is no need to apply an even coat of paint, as mineral wagons got hammered in everyday use. Just dab it on so that the base colour shows through in patches; on some wagons, paint up the sides to give a 'load line' above which the paintwork is less damaged.

Most wooden wagon interiors appear to have been unpainted and to replicate this use a mix of Humbrol matt 103 and 119 or 121, again flooded on with some of the colour wiped off to give an almost translucent finish. Streaks and runs can be added as before. Use this mix to simulate unpainted replacement planks on wagons and vans. When dry, tone down and weather with the black/Khaki mix, adding a little streaking as required. There is also plenty of scope for further refinement by adding rust streaks, oil stains and so on, although this will require additional colours and washes. Don't rush, and remember to leave plenty

Even without any further attention, just weathering the interiors lifts these wagons out of the ordinary.

of time for paint to dry thoroughly between stages, or you may end up with fingerprints where you least expect them.

ADDING A LOAD

Adding a convincing load is not difficult and can easily be made either removable or securely fixed in position. It is also a useful dodge if you don't want to weather the inside of lots of wagons. Articles have appeared showing wagons filled with real coal, stone or whatever, liberally glued in place. Be warned, this is most definitely *not* the way to do it. More than likely you will end up with an unholy mess and glue leaking everywhere. Even if you have not ruined the wagon, it will be extremely heavy and unstable and try to derail wherever it can.

For coal and mineral loads, I used dense black rigid foam, left over from packaging, although at a pinch almost anything will do as long as it can be shaped easily and without too much mess. Cut into a block that will fit into the wagon – depending on the thickness of the foam you may need to glue two or three layers together, but this can be done on the kitchen table. Once dry, the block can be shaped and if necessary painted the base colour of the load – black for coal, Red Oxide for iron ore and so on. Leave to dry,

then apply PVA glue and sprinkle coal (or whatever) and leave to dry again thoroughly. You may need to repeat the process two or three times to build up a good covering, but doing two or three or more loads together will save time. Spot-fix any 'holes' in the load with a drop of glue. Finally, fit into the wagon – there is no need to glue it in, as there should be enough 'give' in the foam to grip the wagon sides and prevent the load falling out. The same method is used for coaling tenders on steam locomotives.

Sometimes real coal just does not look like coal. There are coal substitutes available (although designed for 4mm modellers), which I use in 7mm scale either on its own, or mixed with larger lumps of the real stuff to represent different grades of coal. I regularly use Greenscene's (GS308), although there are other makes that are just as good. A final point about coal wagons – when empty, they would be swept out ready for the next load, which might be totally different to that carried previously. Instructions were regularly issued to staff on the importance of carrying this out, so do not be tempted to model coal left in the corners or bottom of a wagon – coal merchants were most certainly not known for leaving any of this valuable commodity in an otherwise empty wagon.

Adding a load to steel or wooden open wagons is a simple job – discarded foam packaging forms the basis for these coal loads.

Even a flat piece of cut foam can make an effective-looking load, but shaping the basic foam insert gives an even better appearance.

The basic foam insert added to a seven-plank open wagon.

Slater's 'Shock Open' with vitreous clay pipe load. The pipes are made up of two different diameters of plastic tube and the straw packing is plumber's hemp. The load sits on a false floor, all fixed in place with PVA glue.

The steel tube load on this 'Bogie Bolster C' is made from styrene tube with the inside of the ends thinned down to a more scale thickness, then glued together.

Perhaps the simplest loads of all – the small A-type container is a Slater's kit, while the larger BD container is scratch-built. Although two A-type containers can be carried on a 'Conflat' wagon the doors must be facing each other – B-type containers can also be carried in 13T open wagons, but were banned from 'Lowfit' wagons.

This 16-tonner usually lives in the coalyard. Empty wagons were always swept out – coal was too valuable to leave in the bottom of wagons – and the practice of propping doors open to use as a platform was frowned upon by coal merchants and railway companies alike. The folded empty sack is formed up from metallic foil.

NOTES FROM A MODELLER'S SKETCHBOOK

I have always kept notes and made sketches of railway oddities and various details that caught my interest and during the 1990s I compiled a regular series of half-page illustrations for *Model Rail* magazine. 'The Lineside Look' took various aspects of the contemporary railway scene and suggested how to model them. Here is a selection of updated ideas suitable for O-gauge layouts. Others can be found throughout the book.

Crossing the Line

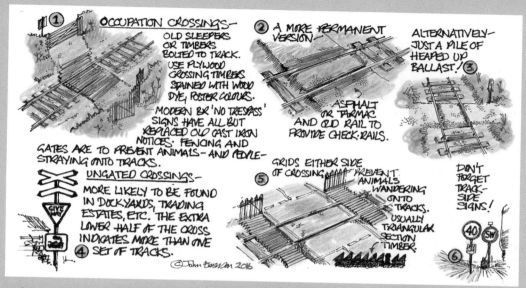

Farm tracks and minor roads often have to cross the railway in the form of occupation crossings or ungated crossings. Tracks in dockyards, industrial areas or trading estates, where speeds are much lower, still need clear signage to indicate their presence to drivers. A little bit of thought and some time spent on detailing can make all the difference. Do not forget signage for road and rail users.

On the Road Again

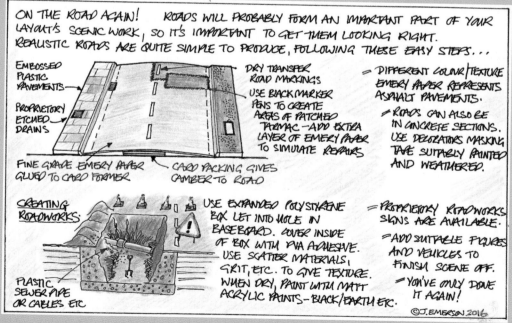

Sooner or later, somewhere or other, roads will form an important part of your layout's scenic work, so it is important to get them looking right. Realistic roads are quite simple to produce using fairly basic and easily available materials, for example fine-grade emery paper for road surfaces and pavements from embossed plastic sheet. Follow these easy steps.

continued overleaf

Lineside Bins

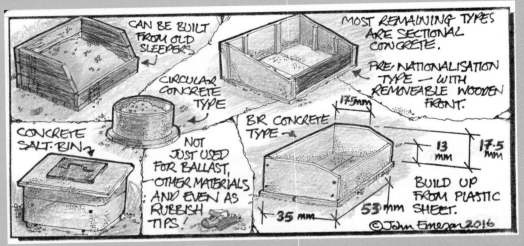

Commonly referred to as 'ballast bins', lineside bins can be used for a variety of different purposes. Their use has declined with the universal spread of track tamping machinery and continuous welded rail, but they are still to be seen, often in a derelict state of repair. Ballast bins are available commercially, but they are one of the most simple structures to build on your layout from styrene sheet, or you can use card and a suitable adhesive such as UHU. Some bins were positioned on concrete or wooden 'stilts' where the land fell away sharply from track level. Finally, remember to add some sand or ballast in the bin for your PW gang to use.

Filling Corners

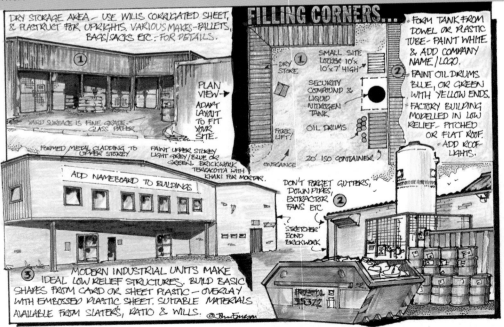

Tricky things corners, especially on an 'L'-shaped layout – on fixed layouts there is often scope for building a street scene or industrial area against a wall or back scene. Contemporary buildings are quite easy to scratch-build and would make a good first project. For layouts set in earlier periods, a siding could also be incorporated in a corner site.

CHAPTER NINE

THINKING OUT OF THE BOX

CHOOSING A PROTOTYPE

There is no easy answer to the thorny problem of choosing a prototype or period to follow. In the end, it will come down to personal tastes or allegiance. Some modellers disregard the question altogether, running whatever takes their fancy, mixing pre-Grouping steam with contemporary diesel or electric and so on. Fortunately, a great but often forgotten virtue of our hobby is that *railway modelling is fun*! After all, it is your layout, so sit back and enjoy whatever you want to run on it. However, this may pall after a while and an interest in one or more railway companies at a particular period in time may lead to the desire to run more realistic trains.

Railway history can be conveniently divided into a number of historical periods (ignoring the earliest iron railways, built before the invention of the steam locomotive), starting with the opening of the Stockton & Darlington in 1825, although it is most likely that the majority of modellers these days will model the BR steam or later periods, with a smaller number modelling the 'Big Four', and fewer looking at pre-Grouping – a period that could truly be described as a 'Golden age' of railways. A system of 'eras' has been in use by model manufacturers on the continent for many years, Bachmann introducing a similar system for the UK market in 2006, although not widely taken up by manufacturers of UK-outline O gauge. A fairly generalized and by no means ideal suggestion for eras

It's more than likely that the majority of modellers will choose the BR steam or later periods these days, with a smaller number modelling the 'Big Four', and fewer looking at pre-Grouping or earlier. In this June 1965 scene at Gloucester Horton Road, BR Standard 4MT 4-6-0 No.75029 is a long way from its home shed of Croes Newydd in the company of 3MT 2-6-2T No.82040 and 'Castle' Class 4-6-0 No.7034 **Ince Castle.** *JOHN EMERSON COLLECTION*

A typical BR Western Region scene as 'Castle' Class 4-6-0 No.4078 **Pembroke Castle** *is given the road with a Paddington-bound train at Swindon, c.1960. Choice of prototype and period to model may well depend on personal allegiance or historical interest in – or dislike of – a particular company.* ROY TAYLOR/JOHN EMERSON COLLECTION

appeared in the May 2006 issue of *British Railway Modelling* and is repeated here.

Historic	1825–95	Earliest pioneering steam-hauled railways
Pre-Grouping	1895–1922	120 different railway companies
'Big Four'	1923–47	GWR, LMS, LNER, SR
British Railways	1948–68	The Nationalized railway to end of steam
Modern Image	1968–94	Nationalized British Rail diesel and electric
Privatization	1994–present	Franchised Train Operating Companies

One of the benefits of following a particular prototype company is that there is usually an individual 'house style' in terms of architecture, signalling equipment, rolling stock, livery and so on. For example, lower quadrant signals, 'spear' fencing, pannier tanks and copper-capped engines are immediately recognizable as belonging to the Great Western Railway (GWR). Choosing suitable stock, buildings, kits and accessories will help to identify immediately the chosen railway company on the layout and give a more authentic look. Proprietary and kit manufacturers produce a large range of engines, rolling stock and accessories covering much of our railway's history, so the modeller should have little difficulty choosing a suitable company and era to follow. Research can become a fascinating exercise in itself and there is now a vast wealth of societies, books, magazines, DVDs and online resources to consider, each covering a different aspect of the prototype railway scene. Whether it is steam or diesel, pre-Grouping or one of the contemporary Train Operating Companies, with almost 200 years of railway history to choose from you will certainly never get tired of railway modelling!

BUYING SECOND-HAND OR ONLINE

For many modellers working to a strict budget, buying second-hand locomotives and rolling stock can be an economical way of acquiring O-gauge models for your layout, or the only way to acquire certain models no longer available. This is not only true of vintage collectors' pieces, but also in the case of more modern fine-scale models such as San Cheng all-brass RTR locomotives. Whilst there is a limited amount still available from Tower Models and Fine-scale Brass, anyone wishing to acquire older out of stock models, or those from the Bachmann Brass range, will be forced to buy them second-hand. Fortunately, they do regularly appear for sale at auction or in the classified sales advertisements in the Gauge O Guild *Gazette* and from time to time in the popular model railway press.

Auctions and online auction sites are also worth keeping an eye on as O-gauge models of all sorts make regular appearances, so it may be possible to pick up a job lot of rolling stock at reasonable prices. Larger and more popular sales will attract more potential bidders, so prices may be correspondingly higher, although quite often it is the more collectable vintage lots that attract big money and unless the fine-scale lots are from well-known builders these prices may not reflect a model's true value. However, remember that items purchased at auction will usually attract a buyer's premium and VAT, which may make the actual price you pay for that bargain locomotive as much as a third higher than you bargained for, so always set yourself a budget with this in mind and stick to it.

It is also good practice to set a budget if buying on eBay or other online sites. One friend who ran a business selling model trains online could never un-

This Connoisseur 4F 0-6-0 was acquired second-hand on a visit to a local O-gauge group running session and has proved a useful addition to the motive power fleet on 'Gifford Street'.

The 'Trains Galore' sale takes place over two days at Special Auction Services in Newbury every December and is a firm fixture in the collector's calendar, overseen by auctioneers Thomas Plant and Neil Shuttleworth. The second day is devoted to fine-scale and coarse-scale O gauge and the larger scales.

derstand why a particular item would not sell when advertised on his website, but could make three or four times as much when offered on eBay. The only reason he could think of was that intending purchasers got carried away in the excitement of the final bidding frenzy and ended up paying well over the odds for a particular item that they could have bought at a model shop for half the price.

Whilst it is possible to view and handle the lots at auctions, this is not the case when buying through sales and wants ads, on eBay or at online auctions. Personally, I would rather see an item before committing to a purchase to ensure that it is in good condition, that it runs (in the case of a locomotive), or whether there are any faults, missing parts or damage. This is, of course, perfectly possible when buying through the Gauge O Guild's Trustee and Executor service at shows, or purchasing from Guild or other bring-and-buy stalls. However, in the last analysis the buyer should beware and always check thoroughly before parting with his or her hard-earnt cash for that elusive bargain.

COLLECTOR OR MODELLER? THE CLASSIC TINPLATE REVIVAL

With the growth of tabletop OO gauge and the onset of World War II, the popularity of tinplate O-gauge trains declined. Hornby and lesser manufacturers

Keeping the past alive – an Ace Trains A4 runs alongside Bassett-Lowke, LMC, Exley and other collectable models on the late Peter Marshall's vintage O-gauge coarse-scale layout. The now established track gauge of 32mm was the closest metric equivalent of early tinplate 1¼in gauge No.0-scale track.
TONY WRIGHT, COURTESY BRITISH RAILWAY MODELLING

such as Mettoy and Chad Valley staggered on post-war, but by the 1960s volume production of O-gauge clockwork tinplate had ceased and it was left to collectors to carry on the traditions of tinplate trains. As collecting became more popular as a pastime in its own right, prices rose, eventually putting the more desirable and collectable items well beyond the pockets of many collectors.

In 1995, having already taken part in an unsuccessful effort to revive Bassett-Lowke, Allen Levy — founder of the London Toy and Model Museum and New Cavendish Books — decided it was time to invest in a new generation of 'traditional' coarse-scale O-gauge tinplate. Ace Trains was born, with the first locomotive based on the Hornby clockwork 4-4-4T

but powered by a modern electric motor. More than 1,000 of these E/1 models were produced in different liveries and other locomotives followed over successive years, including a Gresley A4 'Pacific' (2002), A3 'Pacific' and GWR 'Castle' (2006), and Q Class 0-6-0 (2007). A growing range of coaching stock also appeared, including articulated 'Coronation' stock, GWR Collett and Hawksworth coaches and BR Mk1s, with well over 20,000 coaches produced during the first ten years.

Diecast car manufacturer Corgi acquired the Bassett-Lowke name in 1996 and product designer Len Mills began work on a new range of O-gauge models bearing the famous name. First was a reworking of the Stanier 'Mogul' appearing in electric and steam versions in 2000. This was followed by a Southern Railway Maunsell 'Mogul' (2001), LMS 'Princess Royal' (2002), rebuilt 'Royal Scot' (2003) and rebuilt 'Patriot' (2004). It was then decided to drop loco production, so Len Mills left Corgi to join Ace Trains. Corgi had announced an LNER A3 and GWR 'Castle' that were subsequently developed by Ace Trains, although further Bassett-Lowke branded models appeared from Corgi in 2007 produced by Czech firm ETS. These included a WD 2-8-0 and Class 20, although to the smaller 1:45 scale. In May 2008, Hornby acquired Corgi and the Bassett-Lowke brand, although it is fair to say that it does not sit happily alongside Hornby OO-gauge trains, Scalextric, Corgi and other mass-market brands in the Hornby stable, so now faces a somewhat uncertain future.

Several smaller manufacturers and suppliers have also introduced their own 'classic' O-gauge ranges in recent years and a growing variety of locomotives are available, although most are produced in fairly limited numbers. For example, John Fowler's Seven Mill Models produced a B17 and B1 4-6-0, Pepper-corn A1 and A2 'Pacifics', Gresley N2, Ivatt 2MT and LMS Ivatt 'Mickey Mouse' 2-6-0. These Seven Mill models are based around an ETS mechanism, with Consett-based DJH Engineering manufacturing and decorating the locomotives to produce a 'semi-scale' model. Other modern-day coarse-scale manufacturers include Along Classic Lines, Darstaed, ETS, American manufacturer MTH (Mike's Train House) and WJ Vintage.

The introduction of Ace Trains and the revival of the Bassett-Lowke brand in the 1990s created a niche market with a large following, not only in the UK but right around the world. I'm sure Allen Levy could not have foreseen the popularity with which the range would be greeted and the large number of enthusiasts who would actively support retro coarse scale. But for those who do not relish the idea of an ultra fine-scale model railway, or cannot afford to collect vintage tinplate – or even if you just want to 'play trains' – gloriously old-fashioned coarse scale can provide an ideal and practical solution.

Seven Mill Models V2 Class 2-6-2 No.60873 **Coldstreamer** *in BR livery. This 'semi-scale' model has a cast-metal body assembled and painted by DJH and is powered by an ETS mechanism.*

WHAT'S IN A NAME?

Although there are several intentional but hopefully not too blatant jokes on 'Gifford Street', it is worth bearing in mind that funny names for layouts, roads and shops or factories on layouts may not seem so funny after a month or two – especially to those who may not be in on the joke, or spectators at shows who may possibly take offence in this era of overly political correctness. However, that did not deter the directors of that well-known firm of Norfolk & Goode from having the company name painted on their factory building at the back of the goods yard on 'Gifford Street'. Overall, though, it may be better policy to choose names that reflect the area that the layout is supposedly set in to give it a more authentic regional feel.

However odd it may seem, I'm convinced that a well-chosen name can be fortuitous for a layout. 'Hayley Mills', my old 4mm-scale layout, achieved a sort of cult status and is still remembered with affection by many. I wonder if it would it have been so popular had it kept the original name of 'London Road Junction'? My brother came up with the suggested name change (a play on Healey Mills), instantly becoming a legend in his own lunchtime, although to avoid any risk of writs thumping through the letterbox, I wrote to the actress Hayley Mills, who thankfully gave us her blessing. 'Utterly', the next project and a first venture into O gauge, did not prove to be such a happy experience and for various reasons it all ended in acrimony. However, 'Gifford Street' has once again proved to be a particularly 'lucky' layout.

TEN FREIGHT FACTS

One of the first things spectators notice about 'Gifford Street' is that although it is a big layout, there is no station. When planning the layout the inclusion of a station was one of the things discussed, but as my and my brother's interests were centred around freight operations, it struck us as a waste of good modelling time to build a station. Freight traffic on model railways nearly always seems to take second place to passenger trains and glamorous locomotives strutting their stuff, so it was felt that a little redressing of the balance was in order for a more authentic layout. Besides, the wealth of diversity to be found in British-outline freight stock, with enough detail differences, conversions, specials and one-off prototypes, would keep the average modeller busy for several parallel lifetimes – and that's before you start to consider 'block' trains of similar wagon types. There is also all that lovely weathering that can be applied to make your stock even more realistic. However, there are a few pitfalls that can trap the unwary modeller, so here are ten essential freight facts:

1. In 1959, British Railways owned 1,005,500 wagons – just over a quarter were fitted with the continuous brake.

2. Freight vehicles equipped with the automatic vacuum brake were known as 'fitted'. The bodywork of fitted vehicles was usually painted Bauxite in the BR period. Buffers were either packed out to 1ft 8½in (521mm) or replacements fitted.

3. Freight vehicles provided with a continuous vacuum train pipe only were known as 'piped'. The bodywork of piped vehicles was also usually painted Bauxite in the BR period.

4. Piped vehicles could run in fully fitted trains – obviously if two or more piped wagons were run in an unfitted train, the hoses would not need to be coupled together. It is also worth pointing out that in trip workings over reasonably short distances yard staff would often not bother connecting up the hoses on fitted stock, the train then being treated as an unfitted train running under Class J or K headcode (Class 9 from 1960).

5. The vacuum brake standpipes on fitted stock were painted red – on piped stock it was painted white.

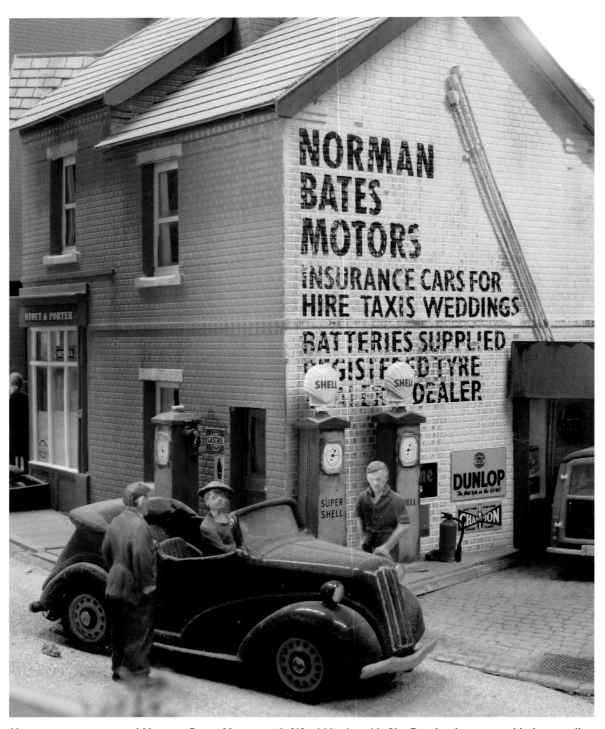

Not everyone connected Norman Bates Motors with Alfred Hitchcock's film Psycho, but we could always tell from inside the layout when someone had 'got it'. The rest of the lettering is taken from an actual garage in 1960s Birmingham.

Fish vans and other insulated vehicles were painted white, although in practice this soon became covered in grime. Following complaints from the Trawler Owners Association, a new Ice Blue livery was introduced from 1964. Fitted vehicles were painted Bauxite, with the vacuum brake standpipes painted red.

6. Brake vans on freight trains composed of all fitted (or majority of fitted) stock had a single tail lamp.

7. Freight vehicles equipped with handbrakes only were known as 'unfitted'. The bodywork was usually painted a dark grey in the BR period, the grey livery changing to a lighter shade from 1962.

8. Brake vans on unfitted freight trains (or where the majority of vehicles were unfitted) had a single tail lamp and two side lamps.

9. Insulated fish or meat vans and containers were painted white in the BR period, although this began to be replaced with an Ice Blue livery from 1964 after complaints from the Trawler Owners Association. However, some vehicles were never repainted, only receiving patch painting when repaired.

10. Now for the nerdy bit – fitted or piped four-wheeled vehicles of 6 tons minimum tare weight with oil axle boxes, screw couplings and long buffers could run in passenger trains. Vehicles with a wheelbase of 10ft or over were marked 'X.P.' together with the wheelbase. A limit of

60mph (97km/h) was imposed on passenger trains conveying vehicles with a wheelbase of less than 15ft – which were generally marshalled at the rear of all bogie vehicles. 'Lowmac' wagons marked 'X.P.' and stencilled 'MAXIMUM SPEED 60MPH' could also be attached to passenger trains. Four-wheeled vehicles with a wheelbase of less than 10ft were not conveyed on express passenger trains.

In general, in trains of mixed fitted and unfitted stock, the fitted vehicles were marshalled next to the loco-motive, often providing a 'fitted head' and enabling the train to run at a higher speed. This was not always the case and especially on trip workings or short dis-tance movements, shunters would more often than not save time either by not connecting up the vac-uum pipe hose between wagons, or marshalling fit-ted vehicles elsewhere in the train – behind unfitted wagons for example. This could lead to the sight of what appears to be a fitted train being worked as an unfitted or partly fitted one. The position of wagons in a train might also depend on the order in which they needed to be dropped off en route, again giving rise to the sight of fitted vehicles marshalled behind unfitted ones.

The same situation arose with the introduction of the twin-pipe air-brake system – connections on the

The brake vans of fitted trains had a single tail lamp (left), while those on unfitted trains had two additional side lamps (right). The 'bull' (lens) of tail lamps showed a red light, with the side lamps also having a white light that could be seen from the train engine.

air-brake pipe were painted red and reservoir pipe connections yellow. Vehicles equipped with the air brake were known as 'fitted', those with through air pipes were 'piped'. Vehicles equipped with vacuum and air brakes were known as 'dual-braked'. Dual-braked vehicles could run in either air-braked or vacuum-braked trains. Air-braked wagons were also allowed to run in vacuum-braked trains (or vice versa), although as the two systems were incompatible, they would then be treated as unfitted stock. This meant that the portion of the train behind the wagon would also be unfitted. An exception was where stock was also fitted with a through pipe or pipes, when it could then be treated as piped.

DC OR DCC? THAT IS THE QUESTION

Much debate takes place these days as to whether layouts should be controlled by 'old-fashioned' 12V DC (analogue), or the comparatively recent innovation of DCC (Digital Command Control) where an AC voltage is applied to the track at all times and locomotives require a decoder (or 'chip') to convert packets of digital information from the command station and throttle into movement and operation of ancillary lights, sound, smoke units, fans and so on. Some layouts, 'Gifford Street' included, have plumped for a system of one set of tracks being DC, the other DCC, thereby catering for owners of DC and DCC locomotives.

While analogue operation is relatively simple, it is complicated by the number of track and isolating sections required and the number of switches and amount of wiring needed to make it all work. DCC adds a level of complexity, in that it requires a controlling decoder in each locomotive or other item of stock (and accessory decoders if you wish to make points, signals and the like work by DCC), but it does not need the same amount of wiring and fewer, if any, switches. It also has the benefit of working sound and other onboard effects. Most importantly, both systems need absolute cleanliness of wheels, pick-ups and track in order to work properly. Also, if a locomotive will not work properly on 12V DC, then do not expect it to work on DCC.

It is best to wire a layout for DCC rather than convert a 12V DC layout to DCC, as this can lead to unexpected problems, possibly from electronic 'noise' in the existing wiring. However, 'Gifford Street' was originally wired for 12V DC and 'converted' by the simple expedient of unplugging the DC controller, plugging in the DCC and leaving all the section and isolating switches 'open'. To our surprise it worked perfectly, although the wiring was later modified for improved DCC working, running a heavy gauge 'bus' under the layout connected to the track by dropper wires. If using DCC on a moderate or large layout, it is worth considering breaking up the layout into power districts to avoid the whole layout suddenly shutting down when a short circuit occurs.

The system used is a Digitrax Super Chief 8 Amp command station with DT400 throttles and a UT4 Utility Throttle as back-up, the throttle being plugged into UP5 panels fitted into the layout facia at various strategic positions. Digitrax was selected purely by

the fact that I was familiar with using the system on a friend's American layout and there may be far better systems now available, but having invested in the system I am sticking with it for the foreseeable future. DCC is only used for powering the track; all points and signals are operated separately either by servos/motors or 'digitally' (by hand) in the yards.

At several shows, the operators on 'Gifford Street' were accused of spending too much time on our phones – in fact, we were operating the layout. This was made possible by downloading WiThrottle and JMRI software on to a laptop, which then works as a 'master controller' on the layout. The laptop was interfaced to the layout with a Digitrax PR3 module via a USB cable and a wireless router set up to provide a local WiFi network – any device using a WiThrottle app can then log on to the network and be used as a touch-screen wireless throttle. This is, of course, a gross oversimplification, but it worked and spectators were amazed when shown how it was all done. Controlling trains at the cutting edge of technology – try doing that with 12V DC. After detecting several unauthorized users trying to hack into the WiFi network, the router was encrypted to prevent the possibility of unauthorized access. To find out more about JMRI visit: jmri.sourceforge.net.

For controlling a layout the size of 'Gifford Street' controller/transformers with plenty of power were required – in the end Helmsman 5amp units with remote hand-held controllers were chosen and have proved to be rugged and reliable in service for powering the DC (analogue) side of the layout.

Brian Daly's 7mm-scale 'Bouverie Peak' at the Wimbledon show – a certain amount of head scratching seems to be going on as the operating team get to grips with running this all-DCC layout.
BRIAN DALY

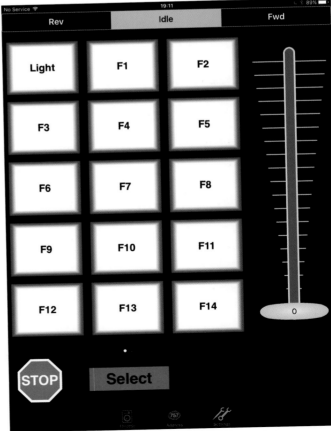

The WiThrottle touch screen on an iPhone has all the relevant DCC controls – the sliding throttle is on the right. In practice, it takes less time to get used to than a normal DCC throttle. BRIAN DALY

Not everyone can say they have an iCase – instead of a box full of traditional transformers and controllers, Android, iPhones and tablets are ready to control the action on Brian Daley's On30 'Bouverie Peak' layout.
BRIAN DALY

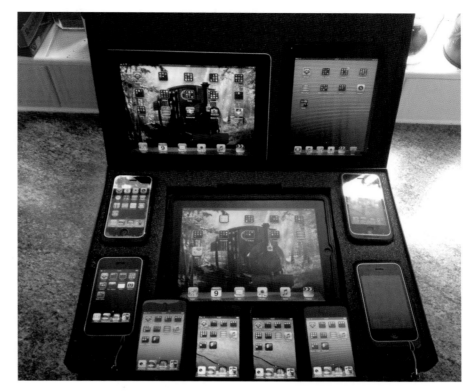

RETRO COARSE-SCALE SUPPLIERS

Ace Trains
'Brilliantly old-fashioned' standard-scale O gauge
Tel: 0207 727 1592
www.acetrainslondon.com
email: info@ace-trains.co.uk

Darstaed
Vintage-style locomotives, rolling stock, accessories
www.darstaed.com

Simon Greenwood
Painting and lining, restoration and renovation of vintage models
Tel: 01729 850842
www.scalemodelrailways.co.uk
email: simon@scalemodelrailways.co.uk

Maldon Rail Centre
Replica three-rail O-gauge track.
Tel: 01245 425413 (answerphone)
www.maldonrail.com
email: sales@maldonrail.com

The Station Masters Rooms Ltd (TSM)
Vintage and modern model railway items
Tel: 01273 453341 or 07963 576526
email: kevin@thestationmastersrooms.co.uk
www.thestationmastersrooms.co.uk

WJ Vintage
Vintage-style locos, rolling stock and accessories – distributor for Along Classic Lines, ETS and Seven Mill Models
Tel: 07711 092477
www.wjvintage.co.uk

CHAPTER TEN

EMPIRE BUILDING

CLUB AND EXHIBITION LAYOUTS

As a generalization, if a layout will not fit into the average-sized garage it can be considered to be a large layout. Whilst most modellers will only have the room to build a modest sized O-gauge layout, over the years there have been many large and ambitious projects, some notable and well remembered, others maybe not so well known. The majority will have been built either by a club, or by a dedicated group of modellers with the necessary available space and manpower to undertake such a project. Others have been built for commercial exhibition use, such as the various British Railways layouts that toured the country through the 1950s and 1960s, or Harold Elliot and 'Sammy the Shunter', whose hilarious antics entertained thousands of holidaymakers at Scarborough and later at Brighton from the late 1950s until Harold's retirement in the early 1970s.

Most large O-gauge club layouts will usually have been built with exhibitions in mind, almost all being 'tail chasers' designed to showcase the locomotives and stock built by club members. Popular examples

BR Standard 9F 2-10-0 No.92123 attracts the attention of enthusiasts on the footbridge as it passes Calvert Street Crossing at the head of a banana special. With forty plus vans behind the loco, this train was always one of the highlights on 'Gifford Street' at exhibitions – by this time, the 9F was running on its second set of bearings! TONY WRIGHT, COURTESY BRITISH RAILWAY MODELLING

'Apethorn Junction' has become a popular attraction on the exhibition circuit, making great use of the 'out and back' format with the station situated in the junction created by the return loop. All this and DCC diesels too!
ANDY YORK, COURTESY BRITISH RAILWAY MODELLING

amongst the many to be seen at shows over the years are 'Ravensbeck' and 'Runswick Bay' from the Keighley MRC, the now retired 'Holiday Haunts' and 'Dainton Bank'. Others such as 'Newchapel Junction' and the BR Blue-era 'Apethorn Junction' have adopted an 'out and back' track layout, although 'Newchapel Junction' also incorporates a continuous circuit, allowing trains to run round for the enjoyment of spectators.

THE PERMANENT WAY

There are also many large O-gauge layouts that will never appear at exhibitions – some are garden layouts like the late Jack Ray's 'Crewchester' lines; others such as Pete Waterman's 'Leamington Spa', John Ryan's 'Over Peover' and 'Bath Green Park' by John Castle and the Peterborough MRS are all permanent

layouts built indoors and not designed with exhibition use in mind. One of the most influential, built at a time when coarse-scale standards were the norm, was the layout of W.S. Norris, which came to be known as the 'new deal for O gauge' and helped to introduce the idea of fine-scale modelling to a much wider audience. Norris was born on 4 May 1893, youngest son of Arthur J. Norris, a director of leading Scotch whisky blenders and bottlers Portal, Dingwall & Norris, which also owned the Lemon Hart rum brand.

Far from being a 'chequebook modeller', Norris was a competent and able builder and a champion of fine-scale modelling. In 1956, he moved to Postford House at Chilworth in Surrey, where work began on a two-rail O-gauge layout in a purpose-built 70 × 22ft (21.3 × 6.7m) air-conditioned shed. The layout was planned to have a northern and southern section (assumed to be hundreds of miles apart), arranged so

Walter Stanley Norris was an early pioneer of finescale modelling and his layout, featured in a series of articles in Model Railway News, came to be known as 'the new deal for O gauge'. Built at a time when coarse scale standards were the norm, its effect on the hobby was profound and had a far-reaching effect. COURTESY MRS HELEN BRIGHT

that the tracks looped around each other into a folded 'dumb-bell' shape. Francisthwaite Junction would be a joint LNWR/MR station, whilst the only other station, Stroudley, was LBSCR with the SECR enjoying through running powers.

Norris was able to call on the services of several notable builders, including fellow fine-scale pioneer Bernard Miller, who had been producing 7mm-scale models of the 'very highest quality and of absolute accuracy' as part of Miller, Swan & Co. since the late 1920s. Other well-known builders were also involved and a number of locomotives were acquired from the layout of Laughlan Rose (a member of the famous lime juice family), including ten built by Miller and twenty by James Beeson. Although all the track-

work had been completed by 1960, the layout was still scenically incomplete when Norris died in 1965. The layout lingered on until 1967 when it was sawn up into manageable sections and sold, along with the locomotives, rolling stock and buildings.

Amongst the purchasers was Colonel Ronnie J. Hoare, founder of model railway kit firm RJH. Many models from the Norris layout passed into the hands of private collectors following the Colonel's death, with at least one locomotive, an SECR 4-4-0, now in the safekeeping of the National Railway Museum. The house and estate were sold in 1968 and so the fabled Norris layout passed into history. Although not quite – until 2011 it was possible to visit the gardens of Postford House, which were open each May and June under the National Gardens scheme. There you would have seen the railway room, although used as an artist's studio, still extant some fifty-five years after Norris first began building his 'new deal for O gauge', which had such a profound and lasting influence on fine-scale 7mm modelling.

THE GAINSBOROUGH CONNECTION

Another large and historic permanent layout, but very much designed with public viewing in mind, is the work of the Gainsborough Model Railway Society. Thought to be the third largest O-gauge model railway in the world, it depicts the route of the East Coast Main Line from London Kings Cross to Leeds in the period from the late 1940s to the end of steam on British Railways and into the early years of the diesel era. The interest and fascination of this railway is in its operation – track and trains came first with little pretension to scenic authenticity, while locomotives and coaches had to work hard for their living. To work the various prestige express, local services and freight trains, operators can call on 150 locos, 100 coaches and 200 wagons and vans. Locomotives and rolling stock are nearly all built from scratch by society members, although some kits have been used for freight stock. Much of the passenger stock was made using laminated card construction, some having been in continuous use for half a century.

With most of the trackwork complete, this early view shows the site of Francisthwaite station seen from the west. This photograph first appeared in the April 1960 issue of the **Model Railway News,** *when editor J.N. Maskelyne dubbed the influential 7mm fine-scale layout of W.S. Norris 'the new deal for O gauge'.*

The late George Hinchcliffe was amongst the founder members of the Gainsborough MRS when it was formed in 1946. The Society moved into its current premises – the old Holy Trinity School in Florence Terrace, Gainsborough, Lincolnshire – in 1949, eventually buying the building in 1963 helped by Society President Alan Pegler, who stood as guarantor for the bank loan. The first layout was clockwork-powered, being converted to coarse-scale three-rail 12V DC operation in 1947 and eventually to two-rail in 1952. Construction of the present layout began in the following year and it now covers an area of 2,500sq ft (232sq m), with over half a mile (0.8km) of track and 150 points. The layout is divided into ten block sections, each requiring an operator to work the intensive train service between the main stations – Kings Cross, Hadley Wood, Hatfield, Hitchin, Retford, Doncaster, Fitzwilliam and Leeds Central.

Midland magnificence – Johnson 4-4-0 No.1757 **Beatrice** *runs into Francisthwaite station with a train of Midland Railway clerestory stock. Taken in February 1967 prior to the layout being dismantled, this rare colour view gives a mere glimpse of what the Norris layout would have looked like in its prime.*

Stroudley B1 Class 0-4-2 No.184 **Carew D. Gilbert** *rolls to a halt at Stroudley station. The line to Francisthwaite crosses the girder bridge in the background.*

Another view of Stroudley station with G Class 0-4-2T No.345 Plumpton *at the head of an arriving train. Today it is hard to imagine the impact this fine-scale layout must have had at a time when the average O-gauge layout was built to coarse-scale standards.*

Kings Cross has undergone extensive reconstruction in recent years to provide an accurate representation of the prototype in the available space, with correct to scale station frontage. Although platform lengths have been reduced, the station can still accommodate ten eight-coach trains. The railway is open for public viewing on selected dates throughout the year and anyone with an interest in O gauge is recommended to make at least one visit, although it should be noted that not all of the building is accessible for disabled visitors.

'LEAMINGTON SPA'

Pete Waterman's passion for railways is just as well known as the man himself. Through his appearances in the press, on TV and radio, most will know that

*Journey's end – the rebuilt Kings Cross terminus on the Gainsborough MRS layout. More than half a mile of O-gauge track represents the route of the **Flying Scotsman** from London (Kings Cross) as far as Leeds (Central).* TONY WRIGHT, COURTESY BRITISH RAILWAY MODELLING

he's a very vocal supporter – and sometime critic – of the railway system and a great ambassador of our hobby. Most modellers will also be aware of 'Leamington Spa', his mammoth 7mm layout. Housed in a large 80 × 37ft (24 × 11m) barn, work began on this 'super project' back in April 2003. Like many of his generation, the steam railway of the 1950s left an indelible impression on the young Pete and those youthful memories are now being recreated in O gauge. A dedicated group of modellers is assisting in realizing Pete's dream, each bringing their own particular set of skills – the only way that a large-scale project of this kind can ever become reality.

'Leamington Spa' is a big project with big statistics – with a continuous run of more than 300ft (91m), full-length trains are swallowed up in the landscape.

On the scenic section alone there are over 100 hand-built points and nearly 180 signals, taking three years to install and get working. One side of the railway room is taken up with the GWR's Leamington Spa station and approaches, curving round to continue along Hatton Bank on the opposite side of the room before disappearing 'off-stage' into the curved storage roads occupying one end of the barn. Leamington Spa Avenue, the LMS (ex-LNWR) station, is also modelled, along with the junctions connecting the GWR and LNWR lines north of the station.

The tracks then continue on into the hidden storage roads. With their attendant gradients and reverse curves, taking trains over this part of the layout demands complete concentration from the driver, as I found out to my cost by stalling the coal train

Regal splendour – Collett 'King' Class 4-6-0 No.6004 King George III *runs down Hatton Bank with a Pullman rake on Pete Waterman's 'Leamington Spa' layout. The loco is finished in the short-lived early BR lined blue express passenger livery.* STEVE FLINT, COURTESY RAILWAY MODELLER

hauled by Geoff Holt's superb 'Super D'. South from the station four tracks curve round to Brinklow station on the Trent Valley line, hidden out of sight of the Leamington part of the layout behind the tall back scene of Hatton Bank.

'Leamington Spa' is very much a work in progress, tasks ranging from easing tight curves in the hidden sidings to construction of the many buildings needed on the layout, with some of the older ones now being replaced using the latest techniques, including 3D printing and laser-cutting. The driving philosophy behind 'Leamington Spa' is that everything must look and be correct – if it looks wrong for whatever reason, it is ripped out and rebuilt or replaced. As an example the grass on the embankments took seven months to get right, eventually using teddy bear fur fabric over foam house insulation board. In an effort to speed up construction, many items, ranging from

platform paving, retaining walls and bridge parts to coaches, wagons and locomotives, have been manufactured. The majority of them have then been made available as kits through Pete's Just Like The Real Thing range – following in the footsteps of W.S. Norris and his 'new deal for O gauge'!

'GIFFORD STREET'

Having already built and exhibited a large OO-gauge exhibition layout ('Hayley Mills'), it was always an ambition of mine to build and exhibit a large O-gauge layout – one day! There seemed to be endless obstacles in the way – cost, where to build it and the time it would take being the main ones. By sheer good fortune, the initial cost was offset to some extent by the sale of the old layout and all the stock, ploughing the proceeds into purchasing a lot of kits, track and other essential bits and pieces. However, despite a

Early days at 'Leamington Spa, before the station buildings were added. The ex-LNWR lines through Leamington Spa Avenue station are on the left with the GWR main line and station to the right.
STEVE FLINT, COURTESY RAILWAY MODELLER

few false starts it would not be until after I joined *British Railway Modelling* and moved to Lincolnshire that the story of 'Gifford Street' began. A track plan was drawn up and a series of 'storyboard' illustrations produced for blocking-in purposes. I like the flexibility of being able to alter something if it does not look right, or even to rip it up and start afresh, as happened with the tunnel area. The layout was built in two phases – first as an end-to-end layout, then if all went well (and as time and funds permitted), it could be developed into the 'full stack'. There would be no station, as the operational emphasis would be on freight traffic.

The period chosen was the end of steam in the North-West in the 1960s and, unlike most 7mm layouts at that time, it would make a feature of heavily weathered locos and rolling stock. Phase One concentrated on the yard area (hence the original

name of 'Gifford Street Sidings'), with temporary fiddle yards at either end to permit a limited train service along the main lines. The main line is not straight, but is laid with a gentle curve of around 24ft (7.3m) radius, with transition curves at either end to accommodate the curved tracks that would eventually be built. Whilst this caused a few problems with aligning the temporary fiddle yards, it avoided that awful sudden jump from straight to curved track that you sometimes see in continuous circuit exhibition layouts that were previously end-to-end layouts.

The first three baseboards were exhibited in a very incomplete state at Colchester in 2003, where some wag observed that 'it ran like a dog'. Maybe it did, but every dog has its day and over the ensuing years the layout has not only enjoyed a high level of reliability, but hopefully also brought

Adding to the variety of motive power seen on 'Leamington Spa', English Electric Type 4 1Co-Co1 D222 **Laconia** *brings a train formed of BR Mk1 coaches down the 1 in 105 gradient of Hatton Bank.*
STEVE FLINT, COURTESY *RAILWAY MODELLER*

a lot of pleasure to several thousand spectators at shows.

For its appearance at the Warley NEC show in 2005 new curved boards and a large set of storage sidings at the rear of the layout were built to produce a continuous circuit with an overall size of 41 × 16ft (12.5 × 4.9m). Whereas the emphasis had previously been on shunting the yard with a frequent service of short trains running up and down, now eight-coach expresses and long freights roared by whilst the yard shunter looked on. Many of the trains running on the layout were based on prototype formations with appropriate motive power rostered. One of my favourites was the Class 3 fully fitted vans – we assumed it was a banana special – usually with a 9F up front and up to forty-nine vans in tow, running at speed. It made a hell of a noise, got all the kids counting out loudly and created just as much spectacle as any express train.

Over the years, the layout was extended to an overall length of 46ft (14m), the storage roads replaced and the inside circuit and yard converted to DCC operation. A large pool of locomotives and rolling stock could always be called upon to operate the layout, although this meant that many different loco types from those originally envisaged ended up running over LMR lines. Eventually it was decided to retire the layout and it appeared in public for the last time at the 2011 Spalding show. Ambitious plans were made to build the layout permanently into a friend's barn, including a large terminus station and reverse loop to give an out and back system as well as a continuous circuit. Sadly, this was not to be as Peter Marshall passed away suddenly and unexpectedly and the grand scheme was abandoned in favour of something less ambitious. 'Gifford Street' now exists as a large

Hydraulic heaven – it's not all steam on 'Gifford Street' and a variety of diesel classes have run on the layout over the years, ranging from early pilot scheme locomotives to hydraulics and more recent types such as Class 57, 59 and 60. Richard Dockerill's 'Western' Class D1025 **Western Guardsman,** *built from a JLTRT kit, waits for its next turn of duty.* TONY WRIGHT – COURTESY BRITISH RAILWAY MODELLING

WD 2-8-0 No. 90492 heads a lengthy unfitted train of wooden-bodied mineral wagons along the Up main and past the yards at 'Gifford Street'. Built from a Snow Hill Models kit, the 'Bed Iron' is another Tony Geary commission built for Andrew Baldwin.

continuous circuit, although with several new additions, including an enlarged parcels bay and new goods yard built on to the rump of what was the reversing loop. Running weekends throughout the year see a regular stream of visitors and a variety of locomotives and rolling stock, when we raise a glass to our much missed friend.

It may be that we are witnessing a golden age of the large O-gauge layout at model railway shows. Not everyone will aspire to building a large O-gauge layout. The sheer cost and logistical requirements of moving a big layout around the country to exhibit at shows, not to mention increasing Health & Safety

*RIGHT: **Happy days – with 'Gifford Street' loaded on the van for its last exhibition outing to Spalding in November 2011, Richard Dockerill, Peter Marshall and Andrew Baldwin take a break for the traditional group photo.***

Work in progress – in the foreground is the extended parcels bay at 'Gifford Street', in the middle distance the new goods yard and coal drops, and behind that the carriage sidings and main line.

Exhibitions with O-Gauge Interest

Month	Venue	Show	Contact
January	Bristol	Bristol O Gauge Group	www.bogg7mmexhibition.com
February	Wythenshaw	ALSRM North	www.alsrm-events.co.uk
March	Kettering	GOG Spring Trade Show	www.gauge0guild.com
April	Hardwicke	GLOSGOG	https://glosgog.wordpress.com
	Leigh	O Scale North West Trade Show	www.nwogm.org.uk
	Newport	South Wales Gauge O Show	www.gauge0guild.com
May	Reading	ALSRM	www.alsrm-events.co.uk
June	Doncaster	GOG Summer Trade Show	www.gauge0guild.com
September	Swindon	Swindon Railway Festival	www.steam-museum.org.uk
	Telford	GOG GUILDEX	www.gauge0guild.com
October	Keighley	Keighley 7mm Festival	www.keighley-mrc.org.uk
	Binfield	Previously Langley O Gauge Show	www.hurleymodelrail.club/show.html
December	Reading	Guildford O Gauge Group	www.guildford0gaugegroup.org.uk

Sources/Further Reading

Boyd-Carpenter, V. and Pearson, T. *Our Railway Histories* (1945)

Essery, R.J. *A Century of Progress* (BRM, 2000)

Essery, R.J. *Freight Train Operation for the Railway Modeller* (Ian Allan, 2006)

Essery, Rowland & Steel *British Goods Wagons from 1887 to the Present Day* (David & Charles, 1970)

Freezer, C.J. *Railway Modelling* (Arco Publications, 1961)

Grade, C. & J. *The Hornby Companion Series. The Hornby Gauge O System* (New Cavendish Books, 1985)

Greenly, H. *Model Railways* (Cassell, first published 1924; revised edition by Ernest Steel, 1954)

Hammond, P. *Ramsay's British Model Trains Catalogue* (BRM, various issues)

Maskelyne, J.N. *Model Railway News* (August 1942; May 1944; June 1957, February 1960; April 1960; May 1961)

Rowland, D. *British Railways Wagons – The first half million* (David & Charles, 1985)

Charterhouse Register 1872–1910 – Tercentenary Edition Vol.2 1892–1910 (Published 1911)

Gauge O Guild Gazette (various issues)

Gauge O Guild Manual

Model Railroader (January 1961)

Model Railway Journal No.43 (1990)

Railway Modeller (various issues)

requirements, more demanding risk assessments and rising insurance costs may eventually deter clubs from building them. However, for those undertaking such a project one thing it is vital to understand is that you are in for the long haul. So put together a five- or even ten-year plan – you will need it! You will also need vision, strong leadership and single-mindedness if your project is to keep on course. But whatever the size of the O-gauge layout you want to build, have the perseverance to see it through despite any setbacks – and there will be many – and above all, go for it!

INDEX